D0439694

Praise for Richard Glover

'*Hilarious*' – Candida Baker

'*Heartbreaking and hilarious*' – Tracey Spicer

'*An Australian Seinfeld*' – Wil Anderson

'*Desperately, wickedly funny*' – Augusten Burroughs

'*Full-on, uncontrollable, laugh-till-you-weep stories*' – Geraldine Brooks

'*Glover is better than Proust. OK, maybe not better, but how often do you find yourself in a cold bath at midnight still chuckling over Proust.*' – Debra Adelaide

Praise for *Flesh Wounds*

'*A funny, moving, very entertaining memoir*' – Bill Bryson, *The New York Times*

'*The best Australian memoir I've read is Richard Glover's Flesh Wounds*' – Greg Sheridan, *The Australian*

'*Not since "Unreliable Memoirs" by Clive James has there been a funnier, more poignant portrait of an Australian childhood.*' – Simon Hughes, *The Australian Financial Review*

Richard Glover has written a number of bestselling books, including *Flesh Wounds* and *The Mud House*. He writes regularly for the *Sydney Morning Herald* and *The Washington Post*, as well as presenting the comedy program *Thank God It's Friday* on ABC Local Radio. To find out more, visit www.richardglover.com.au

THE
LAND
BEFORE
AVOCADO

Journeys in a lost Australia

Richard Glover

ABC
BOOKS

The ABC 'Wave' device is a trademark of the
Australian Broadcasting Corporation and is used
under licence by HarperCollins*Publishers* Australia.

First published in Australia in 2018
by HarperCollins*Publishers* Australia Pty Limited
ABN 36 009 913 517
harpercollins.com.au

Copyright © Richard Glover 2018

The right of Richard Glover to be identified as the author of this work has been
asserted by him in accordance with the *Copyright Amendment (Moral Rights) Act 2000*.

This work is copyright. Apart from any use as permitted under the
Copyright Act 1968, no part may be reproduced, copied, scanned, stored
in a retrieval system, recorded, or transmitted, in any form or by any
means, without the prior written permission of the publisher.

HarperCollins*Publishers*
Level 13, 201 Elizabeth Street, Sydney, NSW 2000, Australia
Unit D1, 63 Apollo Drive, Rosedale, Auckland 0632, New Zealand
A 53, Sector 57, Noida, UP, India
1 London Bridge Street, London, SE1 9GF, United Kingdom
Bay Adelaide Centre, East Tower, 22 Adelaide Street West, 41st Floor, Toronto,
   Ontario, M5H 4E3, Canada
195 Broadway, New York, NY 10007

A catalogue record for this book is available
from the National Library of Australia

ISBN: 978 0 7333 3981 3 (paperback)
ISBN: 978 1 4607 1100 2 (ebook)

Cover design by Darren Holt, HarperCollins Design Studio
Cover images by shutterstock.com
Transcript from ABC Radio's *PM* program pp 189–193 is reproduced by permission
of the Australian Broadcasting Corporation – Library Sales © 1975
Typeset in Baskerville MT by Kirby Jones
Printed and bound in Australia by McPherson's Printing Group
The papers used by HarperCollins in the manufacture of this book are a natural,
recyclable product made from wood grown in sustainable plantation forests.
The fibre source and manufacturing processes meet recognised international
environmental standards, and carry certification.

For Matt and Julian

Contents

Foreword

I'm on a quest. I want to visit a place that's radically different to the one in which I live. This, I know, is the dream of many Australians – people who head off to places like Vietnam, Kenya or Iceland. But I want more. I want to visit somewhere *really* different: a place that is scary and weird, dangerous and incomprehensible, and – now and then – surprisingly appealing.

It's the Australia of my childhood.

I know, once I arrive, I'll encounter a strange country. Drink driving is commonplace. Parenting is lackadaisical. The food, by and large, is awful. The fashions? Well, we'll get to that.

If the country of my childhood still existed, the Department of Foreign Affairs – always cautious on its Smart Traveller website – would surely issue its stiffest advice: 'Do Not Travel'.

SUMMARY
Exercise caution when visiting 1960s and 1970s Australia.

- Depending on the year, the death penalty may still apply. Homosexuality is illegal and may attract a prison sentence. Rape in marriage is allowed. Corporal punishment is applied in all schools. Traffic accidents are common and motor vehicles lack basic safety equipment. Smoking is widespread and is permitted in all indoor locations. Safari suits are worn. They are considered stylish.

Exercise extreme caution when ordering breakfast:
Avocado, smashed or otherwise, will not be available.

Sometimes, when I think about the Australia of just a few decades ago, I find myself doubting my own memories and those of my friends. Could it be true that coffee was a rarity – hardly available in any form other than a spoonful of instant? Did teachers really inspect the underpants of female students, making the young girls lift their dresses in order to check the colour and style? Could it be that women were sacked from the public service the moment they were married – the rebellious ones hiding their wedding rings and even their pregnant bellies in order to survive in employment for a few more months? Did Catholics really find it hard to get a job once they admitted their religion?

And what of my memory of the typical motor vehicle – parked by the roadside, bonnet raised, its radiator boiling over at the mere mention of a hill?

Could it be true, more to the point, that we lacked avocado – the fruit, smashed or otherwise, that has become a symbol of modern millennial Australia and its myriad pleasures?

*

I spent my teenage years in Canberra after my parents bought a local newsagency. My father was friends with the other local shopkeepers, including Gus, who ran the café around the corner. One bright autumn day, in March 1970, Gus decided to pop a couple of chairs on the pavement outside his premises. He thought people might care to take their refreshments in the sun and watch the passing parade as he'd seen people do in Europe. Naturally, the police were called. According to my father, they arrived in force, ordering the handful of chairs be taken back into the café. Gus – Viennese born, a refugee from the Nazis – acquiesced. He understood how to treat a uniformed man. All the same, a public debate ensued. Some locals cheered on Gus, this Che Guevara of the wooden chair. Others encouraged the authorities to hold firm, worried by the risk to public safety of the alfresco consumption of caffeinated beverages. My father was pro-small business and therefore pro-Gus. According to my dad, Gus had survived a Nazi labour camp during the war, so understood exactly what he was dealing with when it came to the Federal Government's Department of the Interior.

With my father in 1968, dreaming of a land with avocado.

All these years on, I'm left with a question: was my father telling the story as it happened? Or am I the one who is bending the truth – taking up my father's tale and adding embellishments? After all, it does sound unlikely: a squad of police officers called to remove a café chair from a pavement.

Time-travel is becoming easier by the moment. I decided to fact-check my memory. I logged onto the website called Trove – the digitised newspaper archive established by the National Library of Australia. I quickly worked out Gus's surname – Petersilka – then found a report in the local newspaper, the *Canberra Times*. It was March 1970 and – yes – the Department of the Interior had ordered Gus Petersilka to desist from placing any table or chair on the pavement, as they may 'obstruct the movement of pedestrians'. Later reports said the tables and chairs were confiscated – 'disappearing on the back of a Department of the Interior truck'.

Trove then offered a flurry of letters to the editor, attacking the department. One said: 'When everyone is constantly crying out that Canberra has no "soul" isn't this exactly the sort of thing that Canberra needs?'

A few weeks later, the department backed down, allowing three tables and six chairs for a trial period of six months, but only if Gus agreed to 'indemnify the Commonwealth against any claim or liability arising out of the use of the footpath'.

The dispute simmered for a while then boiled over in a final blaze in 1974. Disgruntled perhaps by its previous defeat, the department staged a pre-dawn raid. This time, they removed an awning that Gus had constructed over the tables. Again, the public rallied. Again, my father referenced Nazis in his day-by-day commentary: 'The department? They could have given Hitler some tips ...' In the end, the awning was returned. To celebrate, Gus installed what became a permanent sign in his shop window: 'Do it now. Tomorrow there may be a law against it.'

*

So, in this at least, my memory has been proved correct. In Canberra in the 1970s, you really could be raided by police after serving a cup of coffee in the sun. A few months after my internet research, I was sitting in Garema Place, near what is still Gus's Place, with my older son, Dan. He'd recently moved to Canberra, the town of my adolescence. Garema Place is now a sea of outdoor tables and chairs. I wondered if any of these restaurateurs – Korean, Lebanese, Indian – knew the story of the 1970s Battle of the Chairs.

I told Dan the tale, as proved by my research, and he instantly expressed doubts. 'Really?' he said. 'The police were called? I'm having trouble imagining that happening …'

I decided the only response was to serve up another shock. 'Since we are talking about cafés, I wonder if you realise we didn't have avocado. It didn't exist.'

At that, he rolled his eyes. 'Dad, that's very, very unlikely.'

*

Later that afternoon, I decided to do more time-travelling. This time, I was trying to find the truth about avocado. At first sight, Dan's doubt seemed well founded. Avocados, I soon discovered, were available throughout the 1960s and 1970s. In fact, the first commercial crop was planted in Queensland in 1946. I found several recipes in old copies of the *Australian Women's Weekly* suggesting the use of avocado – including a 1972 article titled 'The Experts Tell: How to Give the Perfect Dinner Party'.

It offered a recipe for Avocado Cream.

3 large ripe avocados

1 cup cream

1 cup white wine

Cut each avocado in half lengthways, remove stone, scoop out flesh, being careful not to break skins. Mash avocado flesh well with fork, stir in cream and wine. Spoon mixture back into avocado shells.

Serves 6

Note: For the white wine in this recipe, use Traminer Riesling.

Oh, yes: cream, sweet white wine and avocado – 'mashed'. I wondered: was this history's first mention of what was to become the 'smashed avo' breakfast – that destroyer of dreams, that harbinger of doom, that squanderer of fortunes – now cited as a prime example of the frivolous spending that prevents today's millennials from joining the housing market?

Despite such recipes, avocados remained a rarity. I came across a pamphlet from the time published by the Department of Public Health, which included avocados in a list of 'unusual vegetables' – the department hoping to 'persuade the housewife to purchase them for occasional variety.' On the same list: leeks, capsicum and eggplant.

Meanwhile, the *Australian Women's Weekly* was developing doubts about avocado. In an article headlined 'Enemy Foods', published in March 1972, avocado was listed in position 39, ahead – in terms of damage to the body – of well-known poisons such as baked potato, maple syrup and 'hard liquor'. Said the magazine: 'Research has shown, that these are, unfortunately, the sort of foods fat people almost universally prefer.' This enthusiasm for avocado by fat Australians may be why I was never offered one as a child. No sooner did someone grow one, than it was guzzled by a fatty.

In 1974, the avocado suffered another blow. Abnormally high summer rainfall affected the fledgling production, destroying the small industry that had developed. Around half of the nation's avocado trees died from root rot. The survivors went into severe decline. So how did the avocado achieve its comeback? I made contact with Dr Ken Pegg, a key figure in the industry in the 1970s. Now in his 80s, he recalls attending a crisis meeting with the Queensland Department of Agriculture at which he recommended a planting scheme be implemented using clean stock. The government's Director of Horticulture was not convinced. 'Avocados,' he told Pegg in 1977, 'are an industry without any future in Australia. Just accept it.'

Pegg ignored the advice. Growers in Mount Tamborine were experimenting with mulches, chicken manure and calcium;

Pegg added some science. Finally, by about 1984, the root rot was defeated. By the early 1990s, avocados were becoming a significant crop. Their importance has grown ever since. They are now eaten at the annual rate of 3.5 kilograms per Australian. The industry – the one that had 'no future in Australia' – is now worth close to $1 billion a year.

In 2017, a young Queensland scientist, Louisa Parkinson, discovered a new species of fungal pathogen that occasionally causes disease in avocados. She named the fungus *Gliocladiopsis peggii*, after her personal hero, Dr Ken Pegg, the man who gave Australia avocados.

*

In the battle with my son's incredulity – 'we didn't have avocados' – I decided to score it as a tie. We had avocados. They did exist. But not many of them. And only for a while. And even when the crop managed to survive, the fatties polished them off.

I grew up in The Land Before Avocado.

*

Nostalgia for the 1970s is everywhere. A musical based on the '70s songs of ABBA, *Mamma Mia*, has become a fixture. *Puberty Blues*, the '70s novel, has returned as a TV series. Seventies fashion – much derided even at the time – has a new lease on life. On Australian TV, you can hardly move for bio-pics with '70s themes – the stories of Molly Meldrum, Ita Buttrose, Paul Hogan and Peter Brock, among others.

It's natural to look back at one's younger years through rosy spectacles. For most of us, it was the last time we were attractive, wrinkle-free and had knees that didn't creak. But what was the wider society like? What were its values?

The Australia of my youth had many virtues. To cite just three:

- None of the negative side of the internet – the whole body-shaming, anxiety-inducing, time-destroying project of social media – occasionally lifting our mood, more often depressing it.
- No 'gig economy' – that phrase people use when they are trying to create a hip feel around the destruction of workers' rights.
- Houses were cheaper. A lot cheaper. No, really: a *lot*.

But as I surf in this sea of happy nostalgia, I wonder: how does this period really compare to today? Have we simply forgotten what life was like? Should we be more grateful for the changes that have come to Australia in the decades since?

The Australia of my youth also had many vices. To cite just three:

- Banks, by and large, wouldn't lend money to women – not unless they had a male guarantor.
- Life was difficult if you were different in any way.
- If you were a child, no one would take your side.

Of course, most talkback radio tends in the opposite direction: it's all about using a fondly imagined past as a stick with which to beat the present.

- We got to roam everywhere, just 'be back by dusk' …
- We learnt proper spelling and grammar – with proper discipline in the classroom …
- There was more sunshine back then, and the opposite sex was better looking.

Well, you get the idea.

In a recent survey, Australians were asked the question: is the world better or worse than it was 50 years ago? Older Australians were particularly likely to say the past was a paradise: only 40 per cent of those 50 and older said life was better than it had been in 1967. This despite a lift of 12 years in life expectancy between 1965 and now – from 70.8 years in 1967 to 82.4 years. Plus a sharp lift in education levels, road safety, the rights of women, access to foreign travel, and a growth in tolerance when it comes to homosexuality, religion, race …

*

My quest was starting to take form. Was this a golden time compared to today? Or was it a bit shit? To find out, I'd have to time-travel through that lost continent, the era of my childhood, with all its attendant dangers and delights. It was the period that spanned the late '60s and the early '70s. Say: 1965 to 1975 – from when I was seven to when I was seventeen.

Perhaps you'd like to come along.

CHAPTER ONE

Parents, Teachers and the Locked Stationery Cupboard

A few years ago, I wrote a memoir in which I described my parents. I thought it was a fairly bizarre tale. My mother left our family when I was 14, running off with my English teacher from school, whom she'd met at parent–teacher night. My mother's disappearance caused my father so much heartbreak that he left the household as well, at least for a time. In the book, I quoted one of my schoolfriends: 'Richard never really left home; home left him.' Here's my other good line from the book: 'I was never their favourite. Which is hard when you are an only child.' I was inordinately pleased with that line – pleasure, I'm sure, connected with extracting a useful piece of ore from the sad grey tailings of my adolescence.

Once the book was published, the most common response to my *fabulous* anecdotes was: 'Mate, that's nothing.' Readers would compete to tell me florid stories of parents who were inattentive, uninterested, violent or just plain odd. Of course, parenting isn't perfect now, but at least the grown-ups of today have a sense of what being a parent *should* involve: connection, interest, kindness, a feeling of safety.

Some praise the parents of the past – saying they let kids do their own thing, roaming the neighbourhood until dusk. 'They weren't like today's helicopter parents', say a chorus of voices on talkback radio. 'They let children do their own thing.'

The implication is that the parents of the past had carefully assessed the local risk levels, then decided to build their child's 'resilience' by giving them their freedom. I reckon that's fanciful. The parents were just busy – most of them – with their own preoccupations. Mothers and fathers didn't usually drive their children to sport, nor did they watch the game. You cycled to the oval, played and cycled home. Some hours later, someone might think to ask, 'Did you win?' It was the same for dental appointments, piano practice or finding your way to another kid's birthday party. It's true you learned independence; it's also true that, for some kids of the '60s, life was a bit lonely.

The filmmaker Stephan Elliott has a good phrase for this: it was the era, he says, before the three S's – seatbelts, sunscreen and the supervision of children: 'If you drank enough cask wine, it was almost like you didn't have kids.'

*

'Yes … but,' say those who idolise the past. They talk with passion of the glories of an Australian youth – that is, the one free of the intrusions of today's helicopter parents. Some of this is true. Our parents did let us wander in the woods unsupervised. Playgrounds offered super-duper swings on which you could hurtle through the air. And, in many families, there'd be an uncle with a farm who'd put the kids in the back of the ute and give them a thrill with a bit of circle work in the dam paddock, the kids laughing as they flew from one side of the vehicle to the other.

But here's the reality: some kids did fall off the swing. Or died in the unfenced backyard pool. Or were abused in those woods – the habit of disbelieving the child, always siding with the teacher or the scout master or the priest, providing a free ticket to generations of abusers. Yes, it was fun to be a kid if your uncle threw you in the back of the ute when he did circle work; it was fun, if you didn't fall out. Some kids did.

There's a famous quote about history: it's written by the victors. In terms of the '70s, maybe it's written by the survivors.

You couldn't really blame people for this careless attitude to parenting. Many of the mothers and fathers were little more than kids themselves. People married young. In 1974, for example, the average age of an Australian bride was 20.9 years; her groom was 23. Children followed pretty swiftly; the typical first-time mother was 24. Only 16 per cent of the couples had lived together before marriage, compared to 81 per cent now. They may have had a bit on their plate.

Certainly, a common response to the arrival of children was to put them in their place. There were two favourite phrases used at the time: 'Don't get too big for your boots' and 'No one likes a big-noter'. One of these phrases, or more commonly both, would greet any achievement. The boast 'I got 99 out of 100 for maths,' was nearly always met with the rejoinder, 'So where did you lose the mark?'

Praising children directly was a bad idea, according to the parenting expert employed by the *Australian Women's Weekly*. 'Direct praise of personality, like direct sunlight, is uncomfortable and blinding,' he wrote in the issue of 28 January 1970, adding the observation: 'It is embarrassing to be told one is wonderful, angelic, generous and humble.'

Bragging was not allowed, nor was any form of complaint. This was true in all homes, but the ban was imposed in a particularly fierce way in ours, at least up to the time of my mother's departure:

Mum, it's terrible, I've just fallen off my bike and gashed my leg,
which is now bleeding horribly.
—Well, just think what a lucky boy you are to have a bike from
which to fall.

You'll notice my mother at work: more effort placed in achieving the proper grammatical construction than in fetching a bandage to staunch the river of blood.

The idea that you were 'a lucky boy' or 'a lucky girl' was a theme that would continue to be emphasised during dinner. On the relatively rare occasions our family ate together, we'd enjoy a bowl of Brussels sprouts that had been boiled for three months, served with a lamb chop that had suffered nuclear annihilation. Hence the conversation:

May I leave the table?
—You haven't eaten your Brussels sprouts. There are starving
children in China who would love those Brussels sprouts.

How this plate of disintegrating vegetable material, barely identifiable, was to be transported 5,000 miles north remained a mystery. It was hard, also, to imagine the conversation in Sichuan Province when the generously dispatched parcel finally arrived.

Honourable father, what have we been sent by our Australian friends?

—It is four Brussels sprouts, dear son, two of them cut in half and picked at by a rather anxious ten-year-old. They appear to have been cooked for a thousand years. We must celebrate.

Physical punishment was also meted out at a moment's notice. People would say to their children: 'Come here this instant. I'm going to wash your mouth out with soap and water.' Or, worse, they delivered a similar message with plenty of ominous notice: 'Just wait until your father gets home.' I have a vivid memory of being at a friend's house when both these punishments were delivered – the mother wrenching the child's head towards the basin in the bathroom, before violently inserting the bar of soap into his mouth. Once she'd finished, leaving the boy a blubbering mess, she delivered the coup de grâce: 'Just wait until your father gets home.' This, I gathered, would involve the boy being struck repeatedly on the naked buttocks with his father's belt.

He ended up a car thief. This is hearsay and from 30 years ago, but I believe it.

It's true that the children of the past didn't race around the pub bistro disturbing other customers, in the manner of today's youngsters, but that's because most of them were outside the pub, sitting in the back seat of the Holden, hoping that someone might think of popping out with a glass of lemonade. The half-pissed father, who'd stagger out with the drink usually seconds before his offspring died of heatstroke, would be the one driving home, two hours later, when he was completely pissed. Or 'legless', as we phrased it in the kindly way of the time. Ah, the good old days.

The parents of this period also made good use of what was known as the 'cautionary tale'. This was a fanciful story told to children to keep them in a state of docile obedience. For example, a child who complained when his mother used a flannel to clean out his ears, would be told: 'If I don't clean out your ears, potatoes will grow in there.'

Admittedly, the kids of the time should have questioned the science behind this statement, but – since they were only six years old – they just got on with imagining the potatoes taking root, sprouting, then tumbling out of their ears like a hideous, cancerous growth. Maybe that's why so many of my generation ended up on drugs: having begun life imagining potatoes growing out our ears, the delusions of heroin and LSD must have seemed like a doddle.

Actually, the potatoes were the least of it. If you were caught picking your nose, you might be told that your skull was about to collapse inwards, due to the excavation of so much of the internal stuffing. I'm all for trying to instil good manners – but really? A collapsing skull? Who's your dad? Hieronymus Bosch?

Other cautionary tales were less horrific, and possibly in the public interest. I was part of the generation of children told that a certain chemical had been added to all the swimming pools in the nation. If you urinated while swimming, the water would turn bright purple and everyone would be aware of your crime. I believed this story to be accurate until, well, I'd rather not say. All the same, 48 is quite an age to discover your parents were filthy liars.

Other stories in widespread circulation in the late 1960s are almost too horrific to relate. An example, the tale of 'The Child who Started Crying and Found They Couldn't Stop.' You can picture the scene. Water from the child's tears start to pool on the floor. As the tears keep flowing, they begin to fill the house. Then the house starts TO FLOAT AWAY. Soon the whole village is engulfed by flood waters caused by the little child's tears – neighbouring houses ripped from their foundations, the town hall washed to pieces, villagers left dead, their bloated corpses strewn through the streets.

Okay, I've added the bit about the bloated corpses, but the rest is as told. The story ended this way: 'So you can imagine everyone was very angry with that little boy for not being able to stop crying.'

Who was coming up with this stuff? The Therapists' Guild? The Psychoanalytical Society? Did they circulate this material as a means of drumming up future work?

*

All my schoolfriends had families as odd as my own. One, David, lived with his widowed mother, but she stayed in the house while he took possession of a mould-ridden converted garage out the back. Within that refuge, he played classical music endlessly, instructing his only-half-listening friend (me) as to its virtues. Despite my indifference, I still find myself listening to a snatch of something on the radio and hearing David's voice intoning, 'That's Benjamin Britten, a passage from *Peter Grimes*.'

The two of us would only enter the house for meals. David's mother had no interest in cooking, but had made a fair study of drinking heavily. She'd stir the chicken stew while smoking her head off, slumped wearily against the stove. Accidents do happen. The meals were delicious, but you'd have to tread carefully. Just as when eating a chicken dish, you can end up with a fan of bones around the side of the plate, so here you'd end up with a tidy row of cigarette butts, all of which had fallen from his mother's lips while she stirred. To be honest, David and I didn't mind. We were grateful for the meal, and for his mum's efforts.

She was nothing, though, if not a creative thinker. The wine cask had recently been developed and she had a box of moselle perpetually on the go. The only problem: so unquenchable was her thirst that she worried she was putting too much pressure on the fridge's motor, what with all that opening and closing of the door. I remember being in the kitchen, alongside her son, during a visit by the fridge repairman. She asked whether it wouldn't be possible to cut a hole in the side of the fridge through which the cask nozzle could permanently poke, allowing her unfettered access to refreshments without the accompanying drain on her electricity. The kindly repairman, I recall, politely praised her creativity but explained that the padded thickness of the fridge walls made the idea, while visionary, impossible to implement.

Just as insane, yet in a more conventional way, were the parents of another friend. I'll call him Peter. Peter's parents were English like mine, but of the jolly-hockey-sticks variety. The family would go hiking, skiing, boating and camping. Waste was frowned on and slouching was not allowed. Peter's father was tall and straight-backed, and had been a district officer in Kenya. It was like having Robert Baden Powell as your father. I remember going home with Peter after school one day and him taking two slices of bread from the packet, buttering them and suggesting we have one each. His mother walked in during the consequent frenzy of bread-eating and said she simply couldn't believe what she was seeing. She wasn't angry, so much as distressed. 'You've been stealing again, haven't you?' she said with a stifled sob, gesturing at the opened loaf.

She marched out of the kitchen, slammed her own front door and headed out into the street. Peter ran after her, the pair heading down Mugga Way, my friend shouting his apology for his bread-based criminality: 'Mum, I'm so sorry.'

This memory, I should explain for younger readers, is – miserably, excoriatingly, embarrassingly – completely true. Even middle-class families were tight for funds. Or, at very least, they thought they were.

*

If the parents of that time were odd, so were the teachers. Time-travel to the Australian schoolyard of the 1970s and here's one of the first things you'll notice: your body was not your own. Hair had to be of a certain length. Body markings were banned. At my school, the uniform featured a poo-brown jacket over poo-brown pants. The shirt was a slightly paler poo colour, as if we were enacting the various stages of an attack of diarrhoea. At other schools there were boys in kilts and knee-length socks, or girls in pink blouses with giant pink bows. Some private schools insisted on boaters, as if one were about to go punting on the river at Cambridge.

No variations to uniforms were permitted; in fact, uniforms seemed designed with the aim of making teenagers look as unattractive as possible, presumably in a bid to prevent teenage pregnancies.

In terms of personal modesty, we weren't allowed any. In private girls' schools, there were regular clothing inspections to check students were wearing underpants of the correct style and colour. In some schools, the girls were required to hold up the side of their dresses as the teacher walked along the row; in other establishments, a mirror was used to look up their skirts; in yet others, a prefect would be stationed under a flight of metal steps in order to look up the dresses of the junior girls as they descended. Tell anyone under 40 these stories, and they will stare at you in frank disbelief. 'No way. That is so wrong. Why weren't the teachers arrested?'

Did anything as creepy happen to the boys? I've asked around and can only offer this: in some private schools, if you forgot to bring your swimming costume, the punishment would be to train in the nude, splashing away alongside your covered-up classmates. Apparently, the punishment worked a treat and the swimming costume would never be forgotten again. Oh, and at army cadet camp – at least on some occasions – students were required to wear boots, an overcoat and nothing else, with each teenager instructed to open the greatcoat like a flasher so he could be inspected by the warrant officer. 'Occasionally the officer would make a sarcastic comment that today would lead to public outrage,' recalled my informant, still troubled by what happened, 'and yet it was regarded as normal.'

It was a world that appears organised for the gratification of paedophiles.

Certainly, there did seem an inordinate fondness for nudity in the private schools of the 1960s and 1970s. In those with boarders, communal showers were common. Female students, I have it on good authority, had the added complication of 'that time of the month' during which they were prevented from showering with the other girls – the details of one's period and its length recorded in a large ledger, operated by the sports mistress.

Teachers, as with the parents of the time, had a taste for physical punishment, often of a bizarre kind. Like most students, I was caned regularly, receiving 'six of the best', or 'six cuts', as we called them at the time. My crime was always the same: smoking. It didn't seem to strike anybody that the punishment was having no impact on my nicotine addiction: the canings continued regularly through all six years of my high school education.

At least my regular floggings were accomplished with a standard cane. In other schools, all manner of implements were used – thick leather straps, whips, rulers, sticks, T-squares, old sneakers. Nor was it necessary to have done anything wrong in order to earn a beating. One friend tells the story of day one, third year of senior school, and the teacher caning the whole form – three cuts on each boy's hand. 'That's what will happen if you do anything wrong,' he said, as he administered the punishment to each child in turn. There were 110 boys in the form, so 330 whacks of the cane.

'He must have been fit!' I said to my friend with a smile, but my levity was firmly rejected.

'That man was a malevolent bastard,' said my pal, himself a teacher, his bitterness still evident after all these years.

Some punishments were more complicated. During an episode of James Valentine's *Head Room* podcast, students and teachers described some of the techniques that were common in Australian schools of the 1970s, many of them taught in teachers' college as World's Best Practice in the management of students. Among them:

- Instruct the child to stand on his toes and press his nose onto a circle that has been marked on the blackboard. If he moves or talks, cane the back of his legs.
- Instruct the child to stand facing the wall, but in a crucifix position with a text book in each hand. If he moves or talks, cane the back of his legs.
- Instruct the child to kneel on the floor and place his head inside a metal rubbish bin. Kick the bin regularly as you walk past.
- Force students to do 10 push-ups on a gravel path, but with their hands formed as fists. This will usually cause their knuckles to bleed.

Two of James's callers mentioned how, in primary school, naughty boys were required to spend the rest of the day dressed as girls. In one school, this meant wearing bobby pins and bows in their hair. At another, the staffroom was equipped with a dress they forced the boy to wear, complete with a choice of wigs.

Could this be true? I mentioned the idea to my friend Tim, and he answered, 'Sure.' He went to St Kevin's Primary in Sydney's Eastwood. 'When I was about seven I had my hair tied up in a bow and I had to sit in the girls' class as punishment for long hair.'

Another friend, Genni, piped up: 'I went to a Catholic primary school late '60s to '70s. I clearly remember that a punishment for the boys was to wear the girls' sky-blue tunic for the remainder of the day. The punishment uniforms were kept in the Roneo room.'

Then there was James, who responded on Facebook to my request for stories. He wrote: 'It happened regularly when I was in Kindergarten at the ironically named Our Lady of Mercy convent school in the 1950s. Five-year-old boys who misbehaved in class would be dressed in a girl's pinafore and hat and sent upstairs to see Mother Eulalie (aka Mother Ukulele) who was so old she had taught my mother 30 years earlier. The mortified boy would have to parade in front of the high school girls of Mother Ukulele's class and be subjected to taunts and laughter.'

For the most part, people laughed their way through the stories – more amused than traumatised. Some of the anecdotes, though, came with a real undertow of sadness. My friend Julie talked about the moment, in 1970, when her parents shifted her from a Catholic primary school to the public primary school closer to home. On the day she left, Julie was required to stand in front of the class while her fellow students dropped to their knees to pray for her soul. 'I felt incredibly embarrassed and isolated,' she now remembers. 'It was designed to humiliate me and to shame my parents.' Julie was 11 years old.

One contributor to the Valentine podcast tells a story about much younger kids – two kindergarten children caught spitting in the playground. They were brought before the class, berated, and then given a bucket. They were told they would not be allowed to return to the classroom until they had filled the bucket full of spit. By the time the two children were allowed to return to the classroom, they were both sobbing, as they had been unable to produce anything more than splash of saliva.

They were probably five years old.

*

Many of my own teachers in primary school looked as if they were about to drop dead, but Mr Wiggins was the only one who did so – escaping the mortal coil, professionally enough, during the school holidays. I think we all felt a little cheated that he hadn't waited a week or two and died in front of us, especially as we believed we'd had a hand in his demise.

Admittedly, he was not well. None of the teaching staff were well. The school specialised in hiring the aged and the infirm, but no one was as old as Mr Wiggins, who appeared to teach the gold rush with inside knowledge. He wore baggy suits over a thinning frame and smelt funny. He also seemed to regard the recent introduction of decimalisation as an unnecessary imposition with which, at his age, he shouldn't be troubled. He was limited in his discipline regime only by the fact that he needed his walking stick for support. He could only take a swing at you if he could find an anchorage point onto which he could hang for support.

Mr Wiggins had been harried to his death through a variety of means. It is not for me, this long after the event, to apportion blame, but any competent police investigation would have made mention of the disappearing cane, the rabbit ears and the penis.

To take them one at a time. We would regularly post his cane into a small hole in the boarded-up fireplace in the corner of the classroom, requiring the handyman to arrive, remove the panel, retrieve the cane and replace the panel – a task that usefully consumed at least 40 minutes of class time. The perpetually missing cane would be a source of constant frustration, since Mr Wiggins' desire to thrash small boys was insatiable – for example, when Rodney Box drew a picture of a penis on his blackboard; or when one of the other 30 children in the room stood behind this poor, aged and infirm man and waggled their fingers behind his head to give him rabbit ears. At this point, Mr Wiggins would develop the perfectly reasonable ambition of thrashing the offender, and so would hobble this way and that around the classroom, urgently seeking his cane, only to realise it had once again been posted into the fireplace.

No wonder that during the holidays that separated term one and term two, Mr Wiggins elected to choose the sweet embrace of death.

His replacement was rather worse: a short pugnacious man who formed the view that humour was the best way to tame the class. The humour took the form of tormenting a boy from a Yugoslav family, whose English was poor but whose farting was prodigious. Each time the boy farted, or was alleged to have farted, he was required to place his pocket money into a jar on the teacher's desk. This was then used to buy a can of air-freshener that was deployed by the teacher during subsequent outbreaks of supposed farting – the teacher circling this poor child, spraying him with air freshener, while his fellow students howled with laughter.

Not me. Even at the time, I didn't think it was funny.

I, meanwhile, was having a go at putting together a Year 6 newspaper, with a masthead created with Letraset and handwritten headlines – the sort of teacher's-pet project that would, these days, win you an inscribed junior atlas with gold edging on speech day. The three-sheet newspaper had a solid page-one headline – 'Gangs Form in School Playground' – and a very reasonable cover price of 1 cent. It sold its head off, so much so that my 200 Roneoed copies were nearly all gone by the time the school authorities discovered what was going on. The handful of remaining copies were confiscated. My punishment was to go, unaccompanied, to each classroom in the school. I was to knock on the door, then stand in front of the class and explain my crime – 'printing a school newspaper without permission' – and then buy back each copy. Mission completed, I returned to the principal's office. He counted the 200 copies, to make sure he had the full run, then walked me outside and burnt the lot in front of me in the school incinerator.

I was 11. Mind you, the headline was a bit tabloid.

*

Perhaps you'd care to walk into the classroom of a 1970s Australian high school? There's a blackboard on the wall and a teacher's desk facing the students. Each student is jack-knifed into a combined desk-and-chair module slightly too small for their body, perhaps as a means of preventing any sudden rush for the door. The desk has a hinged lid, with space inside for a textbook, or – more likely – a copy of *Go-Set*, *Dolly* or *Tracks*, which could be read under the cover of the raised lid. There is a circular hole for an inkwell, unused, but proof the desks may have been around for a few decades.

Each student is equipped with a pencil case in which various high-tech instruments nestle: a protractor, a ruler and an array of leaky Biros. There is also a metal device called a compass, which has a long, spiked arm which is intended to be gently stabbed into paper and used as a pivot for drawing circles, but is mainly used to scratch obscenities into your desk whenever the teacher isn't looking.

The classroom is also equipped with the latest audiovisual equipment, by which I mean a small square record player which is sometimes placed on a chair facing the students. We sit watching it, as the teacher plays a BBC recording of some Shakespeare play – the boredom broken every 15 minutes or so when the teacher rises from his desk, shuffles across the room and turns the record over. Time appears to go backwards. You dream of death. All you can hope is that two flies might choose to mate on the windowsill and thus provide a point of interest.

The aim of any class was to maximise the words spoken by the teacher and minimise the words spoken by the students. An hour-long monologue, beginning with the words 'In today's lesson' and ending with 'Dismissed' was considered ideal. In some schools, students would be seated alphabetically by surname. In others it would be according to academic rank – the best performing students in the front row, the worst in the back row, with positions reviewed after the mid-year exams. In yet others, a bright, compliant child would be teamed with a difficult child, so that each could make the other's life a misery. Then, twice a year, the students – both good and bad – were given report cards based on a series of exams. The good students were told they were 'falling well short of their potential' while the poor students were told they were 'frankly hopeless'. Teachers would also try to outdo each other when it came to witticisms. Often these were, admittedly, quite funny. Among the classics:

- The stick and carrot must be very much in evidence before this particular donkey decides to exert itself.
- The improvement in his handwriting has at least served to reveal his incompetence at spelling.
- She has aimed low and missed.

Presumably, teachers shared their acid comments over the odd Monte Carlo biscuit in the privacy of the staffroom. Certainly, the same handful of comments were bestowed fairly regularly. And, of course, every report – as if by law – had to include the phrase 'must try harder'.

It was a good phrase. Students of the 1970s, most of the time, should have tried harder. Mind you, the same was true of the parents and the teachers.

*

Life at school was good preparation for the world of work. Australian workplaces – most of them – are still fairly hierarchical, despite the language of 'flat management structures' and 'employee engagement surveys'. That said, the workplaces of the past were much, much worse. Among the perils: the entitled boss who'd treat any woman as a plaything; promotion on seniority rather than merit; a blithe attitude to workplace safety; and – this is where I get really passionate – the tight grip on the office stationery.

Let me explain. Not so long ago, at my current workplace at ABC Radio, my ballpoint pen ran out of ink. It was in the middle of the meeting we have each workday morning – choosing topics for that day's program. There was me, two senior producers – Emma and Elizabeth – and a young journalist in her first job: Mariam, smart, hardworking and 25 years old.

On this particular day, I lifted my dead pen, peered through the clear plastic body and saw the ink had been thoroughly used up.

'That's good', I said to no one special. 'The ink is all gone. That means I'll qualify for a new one.'

Mariam looked askance. 'What are you talking about?'

These random conversations are important when you are working in radio. It sounds indulgent, but we offer these stories to each other, hoping we might stumble upon an idea that can be developed for talkback. A chance comment about an unwell child, or a possum invading a roof, or a car refusing to pull over for an ambulance might be just the topic we need in our daily attempt to battle through the thicket of 'the news' – court reports, politicians, company statements – and into the real life of our listeners. It's why I'd instinctively commented on my pen and why Mariam had instinctively expressed her curiosity. It was also why I tried to answer her question as best I could.

'Back when I first became a reporter, in the early 1980s, there was no such thing as an unlocked stationery cupboard, like the kind *we* have. An unlocked stationery cupboard was unthinkable. If you wanted a new ballpoint pen, there would be a designated person who would issue you one. But first, you had to hand in the old pen and prove you'd used up all the ink. You'd go, show it to the person, they'd hold it against the light and, if it all worked out, they'd give you another Biro.'

Mariam, who is usually polite and agreeable, said: 'Oh, that's rubbish. I don't believe that at all.'

I decided to go double or nothing. 'It wasn't only the pen,' I added. 'To get a new notebook, you had to hand in the old notebook – proving you'd used both sides of every page.'

'Oh, come on,' she admonished. 'You are making that up.'

It was a repeat of the argument I'd had with Dan over the avocados and the pavement chairs. These millennials are so disbelieving of their elders. The next step was obvious. 'I'll ask the listeners,' I said. The producers all agreed. We had the perfect topic for talkback. Would our listeners either come to my rescue – or shoot me down?

About four hours later, I went on air and described our meeting: the pen, the ink, Mariam's disbelief. Our listeners cross all age groups, but we have a fair slice of people who are aged in their 50s and 60s. Quite a few of them immediately rang the talkback line. Mariam, in the studio producer's chair, was selecting the calls and putting them to air. First up was a listener who confirmed my story about the notepads and pens. She added carbon paper to the list. Each used-up sheet, she said, had to be presented before a new one was issued. The manager would hold the carbon paper to the light and almost always say, 'You can get another few goes out of that.'

Another office worker rang in. She didn't know about pens. In her office, in the 1970s, they used pencils. You weren't allowed to sharpen your own. Instead, you would approach the pencil monitor, who had a large pencil sharpener bolted to her desk with a rotary handle and teeth that gripped the pencil. It was for this official to sharpen your pencil and to judge when a new one could be issued.

Next up, a fellow who'd been a wool-classer in the early 1980s. He too had to present his pencil for sharpening and possible replacement. If it was a real stub, impossible to hold, the office manager would reach into her drawer and produce a short metal sleeve that would fit over the unconsumed remnant, allowing another half-inch to be eked-out.

I wondered aloud about whether it was just a more frugal time. 'No,' said one listener. 'It was all about authority. They wanted us to know our place.'

I love these occasions on talkback radio – moments when it becomes a storytelling festival, each caller topping the last. Other experiences crowded in. For instance, packs of staples were distributed, but only once you returned the empty box. Next caller: 'That's nothing. In our workplace they only gave out the staples one row at a time.' It was fast descending into a Monty Python sketch. 'Whole row of staples? Thy be lucky.' Remarkably, according to many callers, senior staff filled these policing roles. One fellow, a salesman, described his managing director running down to the garage after there was talk of a new set of tyres. The boss, dropping to his knees, examined the tread. 'You could get a few more months out of those.'

It all chimed with the newspaper office in which I worked during the early 1980s. The person checking the pens was the chief of staff – the senior journalist who handed out assignments to the reporters and then checked their progress. Between, of course, checking the ink levels in their Biros. I also remember one COS looming over my desk, somewhat alarmingly, with some printed-off phone logs in her hand:

My boss: Why did you talk to someone in Adelaide from
    10am yesterday to about 10.20?

Me: Oh, it was Hugh Stretton. I'm writing a piece on
    town planning. Hugh is Australia's leading expert
    in town planning.

My boss: Isn't there someone nearly as good as Hugh who
    lives a bit closer?

Newspaper journalism, I know, faces many perils today. On the
other hand, at least you're allowed to ring anyone you like.

After our radio show was over for the day, Mariam said:
'Why didn't you all resign? It must have been terrible.'

It was the first time I'd ever heard a millennial use a
sympathetic tone in relation to my own generation. It was such
a good feeling. Just think how compassionate she'd have been if
she'd known about the parenting and the teaching, the coffee
and the lack of avocado.

Or, for that matter, about the position of women. On that
topic, read on …

CHAPTER TWO

The Gendered Agenda

My father started talking to his lawyer about his failed marriage in 1974 – a year prior to the Whitlam Government's introduction of no-fault divorce. According to the law at the time, it was not good enough for both parties to say they wanted a divorce. A cause for the divorce, most commonly adultery, had to be declared. It also had to be proved to the satisfaction of the court. The adulterous person was named the 'respondent' and the person with whom they were having sex was the 'co-respondent'. Mere admissions were not enough. After all, an admission could be faked in order to procure the divorce desired by both parties. This outcome – two people being allowed to amicably part ways – had to be strenuously avoided.

So, my father would need some sort of evidence of my mother's adultery – letters, photos or eyewitness accounts. In the correspondence with his lawyer, my father pledged to furnish such proof of my mother's affair with my English teacher, Mr Phillipps. Alas, he didn't outline how. Later in the file of papers, there was a suggestion that my father should join forces with Mr Phillipps's wife, since she had had already brought a petition against her husband, naming my mother as co-respondent.

Here's the letter to my father from the solicitor for Mrs Phillipps, 13 May 1975: 'We would like to have the opportunity of ascertaining what evidence you have of adultery between Mr Phillipps and Mrs Glover and we, in turn, would be prepared to make available our evidence.'

As it happened, the affair between my mother and my English teacher had been blatant. Even I would notice that on days my teacher had a day off work due to 'sickness', my mother would also be missing from her post at the newsagency cash register. She even invited him to the house for dinner once, a terrible night during which my father angrily ordered him off the premises, manhandling my mother in the process. It was the only time I punched my father and I still give my father thanks that he didn't punch me back. None of that, though, would have satisfied the court. My parents, as it happened, waited until no-fault divorce became available in early 1976. But how did people achieve a divorce in the days before that date? I decided to find out.

*

One summer morning, just before Christmas, I drove to the New South Wales Government archives, located in an enormous above-ground concrete bunker at Kingswood, on the western edge of Sydney. Some say it was built this far from town so it would be 'beyond the bomb zone' should Sydney suffer a nuclear attack. More likely, the attraction was cheap real estate for the agency's 614 kilometres of records, stored in rows of leather-bound volumes. It's here that most of the state's divorce files are held – both the background documents for individual cases and the bound volumes of court transcripts. Anyone can look at them. On this particular morning, I filled out a reader's card and was given a pair of white latex gloves. 'Our hands,' explained the archivist, 'contain oils that can damage the documents.' Within a few minutes, I was privy to the most startling personal details of people with whom I had no connection.

There was a sea of misery here; I just had to choose a diving-off point. I carried the first set of books to my desk – heavy foolscap volumes filled with hundreds of pages of transcripts. I had selected the year 1970, and – since the records are alphabetical – began with the volume involving people whose surnames started with 'A'. With my white-gloved hand, I gingerly opened the first book. Almost first up was the terrible tale of Mr A. A. and his wife Mrs M. A. (The full names are in the records, but I'll avoid them here.) Mrs M. A. had been having an affair with a bloke called Mr J. Accompanied by private investigators,

Mr A. had caught them at it. His lawyer guided him through his evidence in order to convince the judge the adultery had occurred.

> **Question:** Did you manage to gain entry to the premises?
> **Mr A.:** I did.
> **Question:** Through a window?
> **Mr A.:** Correct.
> **Question:** Then did you proceed to a bedroom?
> **Mr A.:** Correct.
> **Question:** What did you see in the bedroom?
> **Mr A.:** I seen both my wife and Mr J. occupying the same bed.
> **Question:** And they were in night attire?
> **Mr A.:** They were.

The proceedings then paused as photographs taken that night by the private investigators were tendered, presumably of a dishevelled Mrs A. in lusty congress with Mr J.

The transcript of this, the first case in the first volume for 1970 continued for 119 closely typed foolscap pages – the wife arguing that her infidelity was the result of mistreatment. She gave evidence that her husband would never have a proper bath, which made her worry for her own health; and how he would call her a 'bastard', 'a sex maniac' and a 'fucking dirty cunt' – all these words typed in full by the court stenographer, the opening tale in an A-to-Z encyclopaedia of private pain. It's not clear whether they were ever 'granted' their divorce – 'granted' being the word that was used, as if it were a gift of the court that you should be allowed to escape your misery. At the end of the 119 pages, it was 'decision reserved'.

As I read through the bound volume '1970 – DIVORCE – A to BA – Vol. 93' – the same scene was played out again and again: the 'respondent' caught in the act with 'the co-respondent'.

In one transcript from the same volume: 'I seen him go into the main bedroom and then my wife came out with a white nightgown on …'

Or from another: 'He and my wife were the only people in the flat …'

Question: Was his clothing disarranged?
Answer: 'It was.'

And another:

Question: How was your husband dressed?
Answer: He had nothing on at all.
Question: Did you see the co-respondent there that night, too?
Answer: Yes, she had on a bra and a pair of slacks.

As usual, photos were then tendered, taken by investigators, handed up for the judge to have a perve. The investigator spoke to the photos, confirming that a pair of slacks was indeed involved. As he told the judge: 'I entered the bedroom and saw the respondent naked and the co-respondent was attempting to put on a pair of slacks and a bra.'

In some cases, there are no photos and no witnesses – just an admission from the straying partner and a shared desire to end the marriage. Most of time, this is judged as insufficient proof of the adultery necessary for the divorce to be granted.

I flipped to another case from 1970. Given the volume I'm reading, this couple also has a surname beginning with the letter 'A'. The husband of Barbara A., Robert A., has been doing it with Carol. Carol, the court is told, has admitted the adultery. There are pages of evidence from Barbara, in which she details her husband's behaviour and begs for a divorce.

The judge steps in:

His Honour: Is there any other independent corroborative evidence of this? The Chief Judge in Divorce said only recently that adultery proved by admissions made by the respondents is not enough … as the Chief Judge pointed out, if that practice were to continue people could get a divorce without any evidence at all.'

The judge stands the matter over, suggesting that the woman's lawyer procure the required proof. His Honour then addresses the woman herself.

'When are you due?' he asks her.

In the course of this long transcript, this is the first mention of the fact she is pregnant.

'In seven weeks,' she says.

She's carrying the baby of her wayward husband and, it seems, is hoping to divorce him before the arrival of her child.

The judge is not heartless. 'I will do what I can to help you,' he says. He just needs the lawyer to present some additional evidence.

It's the saddest thing I've seen in a whole day of reading this, the saddest book in the world. I hand it back to the librarian who will slot it back into its spot, among the many hundreds of volumes just like this.

*

The legislation for no-fault divorce was passed in 1975 by the soon-to-be-dismissed Whitlam Government, permitting the establishment of the Family Court of Australia on 5 January 1976. Until then, there were 14 grounds for divorce, including adultery, desertion, cruelty, habitual drunkenness, imprisonment, insanity and 'a persistent refusal to have sexual

intercourse'. A whole industry existed of private investigators who would supply photos of people caught in the act. Sometimes these were genuine; many, though, were staged – a family friend or a professional agreeing to pose in a motel bedroom. Whether the assignation was real or fake, details would be published in the newspaper, adding a splash of public humiliation to the private agony. Newspapers and magazines featured ads for firms such as Dykes Investigations: 'All Types Carried Out With Discretion'. In the *Australian Women's Weekly* of the early 1970s, there was a Dykes advertisement in every issue.

In 2009 when Tony Abbott, later prime minister, suggested a return to the idea of fault in divorce, even the private detectives were wary. In the *Sydney Morning Herald*, Warren Mallard, from Sydney's Lyonswood Investigations, was quoted:

> People had to be caught in a compromising position. That required evidence, so there were a lot of photos of ankles wrapped around ears, for want of a better expression.

> It was not work that investigators relished … it got to the
> point where people wanting a divorce would commit fraud
> and deception and 're-enact' the offence of infidelity – hire
> a prostitute, hire an investigator, to catch them in the act.

Even more bizarre, a woman could be divorced if it was proved she'd committed a single act of infidelity, while the man was allowed a little more leeway. On Radio National's *Law Report* back in 2006, one barrister of the period, John Fogarty, described how it worked:

> In Victoria it was adultery insofar as the wife was
> concerned, but for the husband it was that wonderful phrase
> 'a repeated act of adultery' … adultery on more than one
> occasion and you had to prove that, and of course all of
> these cases were conducted through private investigators,
> and the usual climbing through bedroom windows and
> making admissions and inspecting the sheets and so on.

Domestic violence also provided grounds for divorce but was difficult to prove. Here's another barrister, Austin Ashe, speaking again to the *Law Report*: 'There really was a feeling around that it was man's duty to keep his wife in order, and if he slapped her once or twice, provided it didn't do any great harm, that was part of the marriage set-up.'

The divorce cases, sitting there in row after row of bound volumes, are awash with the sexism of the time. In one case, a husband complains his wife won't undress in front of him. He says she is prudish, possibly for religious reasons, but it defies his rights as a husband. Or from another: 'My wife would never prepare breakfast and I had to get it myself. I appreciate my wife was working and was pregnant but her housekeeping and her failure to attend to the breakfast meal was productive of considerable friction between us.'

In a third case – this is all still from the first volume for 1970 – the court heard about a woman married to an alcoholic who squandered the family's assets on grog. Parts of the evidence rise off the page like melancholic poetry: 'Without her permission, he pawned her belongings. He pawned her frying pan, her radiator, her hairdryer and her wireless set …'

To list all the ways in which '60s and '70s Australia was terrible for women might test the patience of the reader, besides which Anne Summers has already done it in her stirring polemic *Damned Whores and God's Police*, first published in 1975, just at the end of our own period of time-travel. All the same, the sexism of the period is one of the starkest examples of how the Australia of a few decades ago seems like a radically different country. Try any one of these facts on a young Australian and watch as they look at you with mute disbelief:

- Married Australian women needed their husband's permission to leave the country. It wasn't until 1983 that a married Australian woman no longer officially required her husband's permission to be issued a passport.

- Until Australia's *Sex Discrimination Act* was introduced in 1984, a married woman usually couldn't open a bank account, purchase property or maintain a credit card without her husband's permission.

- Until 1984, jobs were routinely advertised in the newspaper in two sections: for 'Men & Boys' and 'Women & Girls.' The former, of course, were much better paid than the latter.

- The job ads were just a continuation of gendered schooling: boys learned woodwork and metalwork, while girls studied home science, in which they were taught how to put washing on a line, how to set a table, and the correct order in which to do the washing-up. (My partner Debra failed the washing-up question during the end-of-year exam. The intended answer as to the three stages of washing-up was: 'First the glasses, then the plates, then the pots.' Debra received no points for her sincere attempt: 'First fill the sink with water, then wash everything, then dry it all up.')

- By the end of 1975, the number of women in the House of Representatives was – give me a second to count – ah, that's right – zero. In the period 1965 to 1975, the number of women in the House varied between zero and one. Kay Brownbill, a Liberal from South Australia, served from 1966 to 1969; and Joan Child, Labor, Victoria, served from 1974 before losing her seat in the election of December 1975. (She was then re-elected in 1980). In the same period, the number of women in the Senate varied between two and four.

- In 1975 *Who's Who in Australia* listed more 10,000 men and only 428 women. In the same year, of 489 union presidents and secretaries in Victoria, New South Wales, Queensland and Tasmania, only 12 were women. In Victoria, 67 per cent of teachers were female, but they made up only 10 per cent of principals. Of the 104 senior officers in the New South Wales public service, the number of women – let me count again – yes, again: zero.

Oh, and one observation from the UK:

- Until the late 1970s, unaccompanied women were not allowed to enter outlets of the fast-food chain Wimpy after 10pm. It was assumed that such women must be prostitutes.

The way the Australian legal system deals with sexual assault today is not perfect, but it's certainly an advance on the 1970s. Rape was permitted in marriage throughout the '60s and '70s in most of the country. It was partly criminalised in South Australia in 1976, but full criminalisation didn't occur in New South Wales and Victoria until 1981. Queensland was the last state to criminalise marital rape: that happened in 1989, with the Northern Territory following in 1994. Each time there was an attempt at reform, the issue was hotly debated. In Sydney's Macquarie Street, the parliament considered the issue on 7 April 1981. The opposition was against the change. John Dowd, soon to be the Liberal Party leader, put the case in the lower house: 'Certainly any sexual problems in marriage will not be solved by introducing the Crimes Act into the marriage bed. However, that is exactly what the government's proposed changes involve.'

The Liberal member for Northcott, Jim Cameron, agreed, calling the new law:

> the ultimate penetration of the door of the matrimonial
> bedroom … [the government members] are proposing to
> knock down the bedroom door and invade the sanctum
> for the express purpose of bringing a prosecution against a
> husband in respect of what takes place with his wife in the
> matrimonial bed.

Dowd, later a Supreme Court Judge, then took to the floor once more, proclaiming the possibility of 'saving' a marriage after a man had raped his wife – something that would be impossible if she'd already pressed charges:

> Perhaps, because of the delicate and intimate emotions engendered in matrimonial relations, she will regret taking action against her husband for sexual assault if he apologises for his conduct ... However imperfect the institution of marriage may be, it is far too important to society for it to be endangered.

When Anne Summers wrote about sexual assault in *Damned Whores and God's Police*, she noted how society regarded rape as one of the most serious of crimes, second only to murder, but she added: 'There is a contradiction between this professed public horror and the various means by which rape in Australia is either overlooked, excused or considered a subject of mirth.'

Summers quoted a study of Australian pack rapes published in 1972 by the Australian criminologists Greg Woods and Paul Ward. What surprised the researchers was that, in many cases, the rapists were unaware they'd committed a crime: 'The pack made no attempt to hide their identities and on apprehension seem surprised by the fuss made about a "normal" activity.'

Summers then quotes a Sydney case from October 1973, concerning two young nurses who'd been rostered to start work at midnight. The hospital was on the outskirts of Sydney, ill-served by public transport. They missed the only bus. Soon after, they accepted an offered ride. They were raped. The judge, Mr Justice Lee, said this:

> It is a serious question to ask, however, when two
> intelligent young women who get into a car in the
> early hours of the morning with three totally strange
> men, really deserve much sympathy when the inevitable
> happens and they get raped … it is like placing a saucer
> of milk before a hungry cat and expecting it not to
> drink it.

The cat reference is creepily similar to the comments made about 'uncovered meat' by Sheik Taj Aldin al-Hilali in 2006. At the time, he was Mufti of Sydney's biggest mosque. He was quoted as saying:

> If you take out uncovered meat and place it outside …
> without cover, and the cats come to eat it … whose fault is
> it, the cats' or the uncovered meat's? The uncovered meat
> is the problem. If she was in her room, in her home, in her
> hijab, no problem would have occurred.

My point: by 2006 al-Hilali's comments sounded outrageous to nearly all Australians, Muslim and non-Muslim alike. Nearly everyone thought they were weird. Well, more than weird. Appalling. But in October 1973, Sheik al-Hilali's cat metaphor was being used by a respected Sydney judge as per normal.

In the case of the raped nurses, by the way, the sentence was two years, with a non-parole period of six months.

*

In any timeline of women's rights, there's the date things change in theory and the date they change in practice. So the timeline says that equal pay for equal work was introduced in 1969, but as every woman today understands, it somehow never arrived. According to the latest government figures, women in full-time work still earn 15.3 per cent less than men. The figure has hovered at between 15 per cent and 19 per cent for the past two decades.

Similarly, if you believe some chronologies, you'd think that Australian banks were at the forefront of social change. Here's a quote from the Australian Women's Timeline, an online resource created in 2011: 'Following a campaign from women's liberation activists, in early 1971 the Bank of New South Wales [now Westpac] became the first to grant loans to women without requiring a male guarantor.'

It wasn't quite like that, not in the real world. By 1983, I had fallen in love with my partner, Debra. We'd managed a romantic relationship with her in Canberra and me in Sydney. There followed a few years in a rented house in Sydney, shared with an American orgy enthusiast, an Australian white witch and a 30-year-old Canadian virgin. Perhaps for obvious reasons, we decided to move out and buy a flat. Debra had enjoyed some early success as a playwright and had actual savings, perhaps $10,000. I had at least 500 bucks. I am unable to disclose the price of the rather lovely 1930s Art Deco two-bedroom Kings Cross flat that had caught our eyes, as it would cause eternal hatred of me in the heart of any millennial who happens to be reading this book.

Oh, okay, it was $62,000.

But here's the point: we weren't allowed to purchase the property. The Commonwealth Bank refused to supply a home loan at the crucial moment, despite Debra's assiduous saving. The problem: the loans officer had performed a close study of my partner and discovered she was a woman. Top marks for observation and all that, but I objected to the underlying ideology. Give Debra a roof under which to fall pregnant – this was the line of thought – and it was impossible to conceive that she wouldn't, well, conceive. At which point it followed that she would automatically leave the paid workforce forever.

Outraged and angry, we tried the other big banks. We received the same response. I took out my rage by composing jokes about the banks, in an attempt to entertain our friends:

Q: *Why do Australian bankers describe themselves as 'terrific housekeepers'?*
A: Because if things get messy, they get to keep the house.

Q: *Why are the four major banks like a symphony orchestra?*
A: Because they are so used to acting in concert.

Q: *What's the difference between an Australian bank and a teenage son?*
A: None. Neither have paid you any interest for years.

Q: *Why is an Australian banker like Storm Boy?*
A: Because the first thing you notice is the enormous size of the bill.

Q: *Why is a bank customer like a seagull?*
A: Because you can make 500 deposits on a car and still not be the one who owns it.

A few weeks later, just when I'd exhausted my ability to make up any more bank jokes, a credit union came good with a home loan. We purchased the flat and – through an amazing act of self-mastery – Debra managed to not fall pregnant, despite the provision of a roof under which to do so.

More remarkably, when a child finally did arrive, her lifelong earning potential was not entirely extinguished.

Q: *Why did the working mother cross the road?*

A: Because she was rushing from the kindergarten to her well-remunerated employment.

All the same, it was 1983 and the Commonwealth Bank still believed you couldn't trust a woman because she'd end up having a baby.

*

To get a feel for the time, I decided to take a headlong dive into the pages of the *Australian Women's Weekly*. The State Library of New South Wales has a full set – beautifully bound in leather – and so, on consecutive Monday mornings, I spent some delightful hours hobnobbing with the Australian women of the early 1970s. Much of what I found resonated with my memories. There were pages of crocheted pantsuits. There were recipes in which most of the ingredients were canned. There were the family columns of Ross Campbell – recording the antics of

Theodora, Lancelot, Little Nell and Baby Pip – which reminded me of his genius. And there were feature articles which, to be fair, were often serious and well written. I found a good piece on Paul Ehrlich's book *The Population Bomb*; a great profile of an up-and-coming actor called Jacki Weaver; and an interview with Margaret Thatcher, said to be an emerging force in British politics.

Some surprises, though, did emerge. For example, many Australian women of the time had names like Barry, Greg and Harold. Was this an early embrace of fluid sexuality? Not exactly. In the world of the *Weekly*, married women took not only their husband's surname, but his first name as well. Their own name disappeared entirely. Even someone as famous as the glamourous Sonia McMahon – wife of the then prime minister Billy McMahon – was nearly always referred to as Mrs William McMahon. She was in the magazine all the time, in photoshoots and interviews and the social pages – usually standing next to a woman called Mrs Burt Carruthers or Mrs Graeme Williams. If you read nothing but the *Weekly*, you would never learn the given name of any married Australian woman.

After making this discovery, I spent about two weeks telling everyone I met, 'Did you know that in Australian magazines in the early 1970s, they only published a woman's actual name if she was single?' There were two quite different responses. Friends said either: 'Of course, you total imbecile, every letter my mother ever received was addressed to Mrs Fred Smith. She sometimes *still* gets them. Everyone knows that.' Or they said: 'No way, you total imbecile, you are making that up.' The two groups differ only according to year of birth. The first group: born before 1962; the latter, born later. Of course, as you'll notice, they both leap to the theory that I'm an imbecile.

Back in the library, my eye keeps being taken by the *Weekly*'s advertisements: so many of them are for pills and potions of various kinds – medicines that will help you lose weight, or achieve sleep, or stop offending others with your body odour. This, it seems, is a society in which the women feel the need to drug themselves to the eyeballs. I carefully turn the pages of the library's fragile copies and am caught between two emotions – nostalgia for the crocheted maxi-dresses, the colourful toasters and fridges, and the melancholy that seeps from the tiny boxed ads:

Toppexin.6 Diet Pills:

'Everyone has a nice flat tummy ... except maybe you!
... lose 1 pound a day.' 'She couldn't stand being a fatty.'
'No willpower needed.'

Limmits

'Have a Limmits lunch with the slim beauty biscuit diet.'

Trim Tabs

'One a day for your appetite to lose its edge.'

Trimolets

'Nothing is fun if you are fat.'

A.S.T. Tablets

'Ashamed to be seen in a bikini? A.S.T. Tablets – simply take 3 tablets daily. American Sliming Tablets – $1.35 for 2 weeks supply.'

Teradec/S

'Diet Discipline Tablets – containing Phenylpropanolamine HCL – 85 mg – and Acetophenolisatin – 2 mg – quell those hunger pains.'

What was in all this stuff? Legend has it, some of these pills were mostly speed. In the case of Teradec/S, the main ingredient – phenylpropanolamine HCL – was banned in the US after the FDA estimated it was causing between 200 and 500 strokes per year.

Sometimes the products promised a solution to a troubled marriage. Here's an ad for Ford Diet pills from the *Australian Women's Weekly* of 29 March 1972: 'Ford Pills can help make you as attractive as the girls your husband stares at in the street,' reads the headline. Then, in smaller print:

> Looked at him lately? Not as a husband. But as a man. Looked at yourself? Not as a wife. But as his secretary. Don't run away from what you see. Start fighting. Get a pack of Ford Pills …

At the bottom, the slogan, again in bigger type:

Ford Pills: we'll give you a second chance.

They were a laxative. So, yes, you could woo your husband, but only if you stayed within running distance of a toilet.

Diet pills were not the only product to prey on women's insecurities. Andrews Health Salt, for example, 'promotes

Ford Pills can help make you as attractive as the girls your husband stares at in the street

Looked at him lately?
Not as a husband. But as a man.
Looked at yourself?
Not as a wife. But as his secretary.
Don't run away from what you see. Start fighting.
Get a pack of Ford Pills and a Ford Pills diet chart.
Trim off a few pounds sensibly.
Then get into some of the clothes, the new ones,
that your husband admires on other girls.
It's going to be real nice, being
looked at like *that* again. Isn't it?

Ford Pills:
we'll give you a second chance

healthy inner cleanliness'. Or better, Amplex Personal Tablets, advertised constantly in the *Weekly*, which 'deodorise from within'. Or were, in another ad from 1970, an 'internal deodorant' – 'Banish body and breath odours the easy, effective way. End worry and doubt. 30 tablets – 52 cents.'

What? I can end worry and doubt for 52 cents? Where do I get this stuff? I go online and discover what's not spelled out in the advertisement: it's all about menstruation. Early ads, back in the 1960s, mention 'certain times of the month', but perhaps, by now, the company believes it has created sufficient anxiety that readers will feel the requisite shame without the need for details.

Meanwhile, other drugs shout for the attention of the *Weekly*'s readers. Persomnia sleeping tablets offer 'relief from mental strain, over-excitement and nervous tension'. The main ingredients appear to be bromvaletone and carbromal – described as 'sedative-hypnotic' drugs.

More commonly, people chose the two popular headache powders: Bex, popularly mocked in the prescription 'Have a cup of tea, a Bex and a good lie-down'; and Vincent's Powders, which, for some reason, were considered slightly more middle-class. Both were huge at the time. In fact, in 1956, Vincent's was responsible for the first advertising slogan of the television era: 'TV stands for Take Vincent's!' Both Bex and Vincent's were compound analgesics, containing a mix of aspirin, phenacetin and caffeine, leading to addiction and, in some cases, fatal

Museum of Applied Arts & Sciences

kidney disease. The recommended dose was three powders a day – I know because we used to sell them in our family newsagency. My early arithmetic skills were honed on my ability to add up the standard order of the day – a *Daily Mirror*, a packet of Winfield Red and a box of Bex. (To be precise: 10 cents plus 67 cents plus 15 cents = 92 cents.)

Both Vincent's and Bex were banned in Australia in 1977 after their health impacts became obvious. Following the ban, the nation's rate of kidney disease fell sharply. In particular, the rate of female pelvic cancer – a disease for which the survival rate is not good – dropped 52 per cent in the two decades following the products' removal.

Bex and Vincent's were, of course, over-the-counter medications. Many wanted stronger stuff. In the year to March 1971, nearly a million prescriptions for Valium were written by general practitioners, two-thirds of them for women. Another 800,000 were written for the anti-depressant Tryptanol,

sussan

take one before retiring...

Sussan's trio of tantalising tranquillisers by Diamond Cut! from just $3.50

Left: Style 4823
Mint cool Bri Nylon pique billowing from a bodice embroidered with flowers traced with lace. White, pink, blue, lilac. SSW-OS. $4.00.

Centre: Style 6800
Bri Nylon Diamond Wave floating lightly from a bib of beautiful embroidery framed with lace. In pink or turquoise. SSW-OS. $5.00.

Right: Style 4835
Weightless voile drifting from a picture-postcard neckline. Pretty with ribbons and lace. Pink, lilac, white or turquoise. SSW-OS. $3.50.

MAIL ORDERS: Please send your mail orders to Sussan at the following address in your State and include second choice of colour.
NSW, QLD—PO Box 126 Glebe 2037
VIC, ACT, TAS—PO Box 480G Melbourne 3001
SA—61 Hindle St Adelaide 5000
WA—719 Hay St Perth 6000

Please include 30c postage.

Name ....
Address ....
1st colour choice .... 2nd choice ....
Size .... Style No. .... Cash .... COD ....

Fashion you like at a price that's right from Sussan's 200 stores throughout Australia

Don't just take a tranquiliser. Wear one.

which advertised itself to doctors as the solution to all sorts of complaints – from 'loss of interest' to 'loss of confidence and sense of importance'.

Weirdly, the practice of tranquillising yourself before going to bed was so common that, in September 1972, the clothing company Sussan played with the idea when advertising its new nightgowns: 'Take one before retiring – Sussan's trio of tantalising tranquillisers.' The headline is below a photo of the three Bri-Nylon nightgowns, each available for the price of $3.50.

*

Why would women of the 1970s want to be so drugged up? Why would so many be suffering from a 'loss of interest' or a 'loss of confidence and sense of importance'? The rest of the *Women's Weekly* provides some clues. Here, in March 1970, readers are writing in on the topic of 'The Happiest Day in Your Married Life?' Some write about children, but others about the proper way to deal with a husband:

> The happiest day of my married life was the day after our
> first big quarrel, when I realised the joy of reconciliation
> and knew the wisdom of pocketing my pride.
> $2 to Mrs C. G. of Beecroft, NSW

Or from the 'Home Hints' section for 7 January 1970:

> As you iron your husband's shirts, hang each one on a
> wire hanger with a freshly ironed handkerchief folded
> over the lower rung. He'll appreciate the time saved
> every morning.
>
> $2 to Mrs M. Rorrison of Edna Street, Salisbury, Qld

Or here's a quiz from the same period, headlined: 'Are YOU still the Girl HE married?' It's multiple choice, and with each question, the reader is offered an option that focuses on her own needs, and one in which she is a doormat for her husband. The correct answer is always the latter. For instance:

> He forgot your wedding anniversary. Do you:
> a) Sulk all day and burst into tears when he asks you
>   what's wrong.
> b) Adopt a rather amused air and pretend you, too,
>   have forgotten.
> c) Buy yourself a present and charge it to him.
> d) Prepare his favourite meal – and serve it by candlelight.

The correct answer is 'd', for three points. The 'amused air' gets one point, but there are NO points on offer for buying yourself a present with his money.

Or another:

When he gets home from the office, do you receive him:
a) By telling him all the problems you've had during the day.
b) In jeans and an old top, but you give him a hug.
c) With a brief 'hello' – you are all wrapped up in some housework.
d) Freshly groomed and coiffed.

The 'hello' is not too bad, but only 'd' – 'freshly groomed and coiffed' – gets you the full complement of marks. Do we still even have the word 'coiffed'?

One more:

He said he'd be home later than usual, but it's one in the morning, and he's STILL not home. Do you:
a) Silently call him every possible name and mentally prepare a tirade, to be delivered with great emotion as soon as he gets home.
b) Phone every police station in the city.
c) Call some friends to see if he's with them.
d) Tell yourself he must be having a good time and go peacefully to bed.

I'll leave it to you, to guess the 'correct' answer. Oh, okay, of course it's 'd': three points. Once the reader added up her score, she was provided with a quick personality assessment. High marks revealed: 'You are really an exceptional person ... he has never regretted having you for his wife.' Alternatively, a low score earned this rebuke: 'Take a good long look at yourself ... you are no longer the charming girl, sweet and understanding, whom he married.'

*

In the popular imagination, the late '60s and early '70s are a time of free love, feminism, and social experimentation: the 'swinging sixties' and all that. Maybe, but it took a while to land in the Australian suburbs. The contraceptive pill, it's true, was introduced in 1961, Australia becoming the second country in the world to allow its use. The caveat: it was for married women only. Unmarried women didn't officially get the go-ahead until 1971, even if many a sneaky prescription was issued in the meantime. Yes, *Cleo* arrived in 1972, but sexual ignorance was rife. In 1975, the gynaecologist Dr Jules Black reported that he'd interviewed 750 women over the course of three years in his Sydney practice. Only three, he said, had an adequate knowledge of sex. 'Every week,' he said, 'I show a woman where her clitoris is – and if her husband is there I show him as well.'

Mind you, according to the views of the time, sex in marriage was inevitably dull. The VFL coach Ron Barassi was once asked whether he objected to his players having sex on the night before a big game. 'I'd say in moderation,' he replied. 'I wouldn't be rapt in a single player having a new sexual adventure on a Friday night but a married man wouldn't lose any energy by it. With him it could be a regular thing and I don't think it could do him much harm.'

*

In the foreword to the 2017 edition of *Damned Whores*, Anne Summers celebrates the progress women have achieved: 'The Australia I wrote about in the early 1970s has not changed totally beyond recognition, but I expect young people today might be astonished to learn what life used to be like for women.'

A case in point: the so called 'marriage bar'. In the Australian public service, when a woman married she automatically lost her job. The policy was in place until 1966 – not as custom, but as legislation. As a result, many women tried to hide their marital status – making no mention of a husband, removing their wedding ring or attempting to conceal a pregnancy beneath loose clothing. You can only imagine the conversations:

Boss: Susan, are you pregnant?

Susan: No, really. I'm just a bit fat. I must stop eating those potatoes.

Some were caught in their subterfuge by a slip of the tongue. Merle Thornton, who worked for the ABC, spent two years concealing her marriage before being forced to resign. The bump of her four-and-a-half-month pregnancy had become impossible to hide. She wasn't the only one: Merle has told of a friend who'd secretly married but was exposed when someone rang the office and asked for her by her married name.

The 'marriage bar' legislation was controversial. A similar rule had, after all, been abandoned by the British civil service as far back as 1946. In 1961, the Australian cabinet discussed the issue before deciding: 'The Australian social structure would be best served if there were no change, and that the Commonwealth Government should not lead in encouraging married women away from their homes and into employment.'

Merle Thornton, by the way, had been an important figure in a campaign involving a different sort of bar. In March 1965, Merle and her pal Rosalie Bogner chained themselves to the public bar in the Regatta Hotel in Brisbane. Like every other front bar, women were banned. In the Australia of Merle Thornton's youth, you couldn't get a drink where you wanted, and if you married you were sacked.

A final note: the Regatta Hotel in Brisbane now features 'Merle's Bar'. Merle sometimes drinks there: 'I'm prepared to pay,' she said on the 50th anniversary of her protest, 'but they rarely ask me.'

I'm calling that progress.

CHAPTER THREE

Let's Eat

In my bookcase at home, I have one of my mother's old cookbooks. It's called *Oh, for a French Wife!* and was first published in Sydney in 1952. Later there were sequels, with titles like *Oh, for a Man Who Cooks*, *The Garrulous Gourmet* and *Cooking for Bachelors*. The books represent year zero for Australian food culture. Sydney, at the time, had a Society of Gourmets. There were six members – among them a couple of Mad Men from the nascent advertising industry, and two foreign diplomats. Together, they were trying to create a food culture where there was none, recording their travails in this series of books. Sour cream, for instance, was unavailable. One recipe in *Oh, for a French Wife!* suggested buying ordinary cream a few days ahead of use, so it would sour a little in the 'frig' (as they spelled it). Fresh herbs such as tarragon were rare – although, we were told, there was one fellow in Mittagong who'd managed to grow some.

If you wanted to make sauce Béarnaise you'd be best to order dried tarragon from Fortnum and Mason in London. Chicken was an expensive dish, but so delicious the authors pledged they were willing to 'travel by tram rather than taxi' in order to place one on the table. And quiche Lorraine was sufficiently novel it was described from scratch – 'this is really an open-faced tart' – and recommended as the 'masterpiece' that would provide the 'climax' to any cocktail party.

Not only did 'real men' forgo quiche; all Australians did.

Sydney appears to be a small town, where everyone knew each other. The authors – Ted Moloney and Deke Coleman – were able to reveal how individual dishes first arrived. Steak Diane, they say, was introduced to the country by a chef called Tony Clerici. There are only two private homes, they lament, where one might be served the skinless sausages known as quenelles. Then there's a mention of coffee, which is described as a relatively recent arrival. 'We are the 'first generation of coffee drinkers', the authors say in the 1957 instalment of the series, 'and as a result we are unsure of ourselves, just as the Americans are unsure of themselves at the present time with tea'. They go on to debate how to make a cup of the stuff properly.

If you read Wikipedia on the history of coffee in Australia, you'd think espresso was common by the end of the 1950s and ubiquitous by the 1960s and 1970s. That may be true for some, most of them living in the inner suburbs of Melbourne and

Sydney, but it's not how I remember it. At my parents' house, we always enjoyed 'single-origin' coffee – the single origin being a can of International Roast, sitting by the electric jug. A heaped teaspoon of International Roast, combined with large quantities of both sugar and milk, produced a most enjoyable beverage. My father owned a percolator, it's true, a porcelain Corning Ware device, white with a blue floral pattern, but I don't recall it ever being used. We certainly never had any ground coffee to put in the thing. Maybe – on the occasion of a dinner party – he'd pile it up with International Roast and hope no one noticed.

Outside the home, Gus – he of the Pavement Dining Wars (1970–74) – did offer espresso, but his café wasn't open past the early evening. When I was 17, my friend Mark and I used to regularly drive the hour or so to the Yass Truck Stop, where we'd gorge ourselves on countless cups of Caterer's Blend coffee – the product that made International Roast look fancy. (Other establishments offered Pablo, over which a discreet veil must be drawn.) The year was 1975.

By 1979, one store in the Canberra Cinema Centre was able to advertise in the local newspaper: 'Tea/lunch shop service is about to include espresso coffee!', the exclamation mark an indication of the magnitude of the news. The cappuccino was even rarer. In my admittedly suburban experience, it took until the early '80s for proper coffee machines to become commonplace. I used to go to one café in Mittagong where the espresso machine was used to heat the milk for a cappuccino, hissing steam with much drama, but the coffee was still a heaped teaspoon of International Roast. I nicknamed the drink a 'cheap-a-chino', and used to buy one whenever possible, just for the taste of home.

A year or two later and fancy coffee was everywhere. Friends bought stove-top espresso machines – the 'Atomic' was the coolest brand – and the 'French press' glass plunger became as mandatory a part of life in the mid-1980s as Cyndi Lauper and bouffant hair. Sadly, due to a local misunderstanding, coffee was drunk last thing at night – a sophisticated end to dinner, accompanied by a packet of After Dinner Mints – rather than first thing in the morning. It was only after a decade of sleepless nights that the error was finally rectified.

All the same, the Australian enthusiasm for coffee couldn't be quelled. The shift is captured in figures from the Australian Bureau of Statistics. Before the '60s, the agency ignores coffee entirely in its examination of the nation's beverage consumption, concentrating on tea. In 1961 it published, for the first time, comparative figures for the two beverages. At that point, just 1.7 pounds of coffee was being consumed per person per year, compared to 5.9 pounds of tea. From then on, coffee consumption rose and tea fell with each passing year. The crossover point was reached in 1978–79 when precisely the same amount of both were consumed: 1.68 kilograms per head. In that year alone – 1978–79 – the consumption of coffee increased by 36 per cent.

Four decades on, Australia is acknowledged as making some of the best coffee in the world. Cafés in other places – London, New York and even Budapest – advertise themselves as having an Australian barista; the 'flat white', an Australian invention, which like every other Australian invention is also claimed by the Kiwis, has now been exported across the globe. And even at that truck stop in Yass to which Mark and I used to escape to have our cup of instant, they now offer a choice of cappuccino, flat white, latte and mocha, all available with four choices of milk – regular, skim, soy or lactose free.

*

Do you want a meal to go with that coffee? If so, you may wish to prepare some food in an authentic '70s way. I was taught to cook by my father in the two days before I left home at the end of 1976 – the high point of '70s cuisine. The two recipes I learned to prepare were steak Diane (for fancy) and Welsh rarebit (for day to day). I have located both dishes in a modern recipe book, and the instructions bear no relation to the way I was taught to do things by my father. His version of steak Diane, for instance, was far from being a complex dish involving cream, chopped parsley, cognac and garlic. Instead, it consisted of a piece of thin steak thrown in a frypan, then drowned in Worcestershire sauce. And Welsh rarebit, far from being a subtle creation involving milk, mustard, beer and a double boiler, was suspiciously similar to cheese on toast. 'Take the cheese, son, put it on the bread, then pop it under the griller ... voilà, Welsh rarebit.' My father's breakfast special – a raw egg cracked into a glass of milk and then swallowed as one rushed out the door – was similarly dignified by the term 'egg-nog'.

My mother had left the family home before the '70s hit their stride, but her cooking was even worse than my father's. Years later, I remember hearing about a terrible farm accident in which chickens were accidently gassed then incinerated, and thinking: 'Oh, Mum's recipe, I suppose.' In the years she lived with us, she only really had one mainstay. It was a version of tuna mornay in which she would combine a can of tuna with a year's supply of wallpaper paste. Unless you got it down fast, it would set. This food – really more a craft project than a meal – would be served with vegetables boiled until they turned grey. There was nothing unusual in this. Most people believed that vegetables had to be cooked until they were in a state of disintegration. In fact, most cooks added bicarbonate of soda to the water so that the vegetables stayed green, despite being turned into sludge. At least it was green sludge. Meat, similarly, was not so much cooked as subjected to incineration. If you asked for a rare steak, particularly in a rural pub, the cook would come out and give you a good long stare.

Another problem: cookbooks today blather on about using the freshest ingredients possible, but this was not the authentic '70s way. Steak, for a start, had to be frozen, and then defrosted. For reasons that now remain unclear, everyone was crazy about buying meat in bulk then freezing it. If you didn't have half a cow slung in a chest freezer in the garage, you really weren't alive. You could have butcher shops on either side, and you'd still buy a three-month supply of meat, which you'd store under a mountain of frozen peas and beans. It was as if we all lived on the outer Barcoo and had to survive for a year before being resupplied. Handwritten notes, attesting to the nature of the meat and its precise age, would inevitably become detached from the parcel, leading to the regular discussion:

What's for dinner, Dad?
— Meat.
What kind of meat?
— Meat of some kind. I can't be sure.

Decade-old chicken was regularly served.

Meanwhile, both potatoes and sweet corn were cooked in the oven wrapped in aluminium foil. Presumably, people were copying the Black Stump steak restaurants, which would serve baked potatoes wrapped in foil topped with rock-star ingredients like sour cream and chives, both nestled in a hatched opening atop the parcel. 'We can't afford to have the house clad in aluminium, but at least we can clad the spuds' was the line of thought.

Over at the homes of my schoolfriends, meals were even more sophisticated, if you can imagine such a thing. Many and varied were my encounters with canned pineapple. The rule seemed to be: when in doubt, toss in a can of pineapple, whether it was dessert, main course, breakfast or lunch. I particularly remember the 'lamb chops with ginger and pineapple sauce' at one pal's house. This enthusiasm for canned pineapple was partly caused by the unavailability of pretty much anything else. Spuds, beans and steak were commonplace. But things you'd now find in every supermarket were considered pretty damn exotic – broccoli, chillies, garlic, basil, fetta, haloumi and so endlessly on. Until the late 1960s, olive oil was rarely sold as a cooking ingredient. It usually came in a tiny bottle, purchased at the chemist – its main use was as a cure for earache. I don't know why people's ears were aching. Presumably due to everyone screaming: 'How am I meant to dress a salad now the chemist is closed?'

We didn't even have iceberg lettuce. Well, we did – but it wasn't called iceberg lettuce. It was just called lettuce. The reason? There were no other kinds.

Seventies cuisine was a land of vol au vents (or vol au vomits, as some people called them), Devils on Horseback (bacon-wrapped-around-a-prune-wrapped-around-an-almond), smoked oysters on Jatz crackers, and Deb powdered potato (just add water). Yoghurt, meanwhile, was mainly sold in health food shops and considered a bit hippy. Beetroot and asparagus were both eaten all the time, but only from tins. Who knew either existed outside of one?

Families from migrant backgrounds brought a more varied and exciting food culture to Australia – a culture occasionally spotted in the sandwich a friend might bring to school, or – if you were lucky – experienced during a visit to their home. One of my best friends in high school was a boy from Sri Lanka, Arun, now a successful businessman. The two of us had decided to produce a school newspaper and, during production week, I'd stay at his house for days at a time. The newspaper was called *Contention* and was less tabloid than my ill-fated primary school attempt. Each issue began with a burning and seriously presented topic: 'Co-education – Is It the Future?', or 'Should Caning be Banned?' We'd construct each issue at Arun's place, sticking columns of typed-out copy into position using Clag paste. A Gestetner duplicating machine, borrowed from the school, would complete the process – allowing us a momentary high from sniffing the ink. Arun's father, a distinguished journalist who edited government publications, would critique our headlines – 'A bit racy, boys' – while his mother would cook us dishes from Sri Lanka. There were curries for dinner, curries for lunch and curries for breakfast – a welcome break from my seven-nights-a-week menu of grilled lamb chops.

Two things stand out in my memory. We ate the curry using our hands, not utensils: Arun's mother said that I, as a non-Sri Lankan, was permitted to get my hands messy down to my second knuckle, while her son must mess-up nothing but his fingertips. And, a second memory: Arun's mother would always require us to grind the spices in a large mortar and pestle, the two of us sitting on the back step of this suburban house in Canberra, in the dry heat of summer or the dry cold of winter, both as different from Sri Lanka as you could find. One time we came in from outside with our dusty offerings of cloves, cardamom and cinnamon to find Arun's mother sitting weeping at the kitchen table, hands around her head, tears rolling down her face. The sound of the mortar and pestle, the clink of stone on stone, just outside the back door, had been too much. Too evocative of her childhood. Too many memories of the land she'd left behind.

This was the weirdness of the Australian food culture of the time. In 1974 Arun could be eating authentic vegetarian curries every night of the week – and breakfast too – and, were it not for our friendship, I would hardly have known such a thing could occur. It was part of the reason that migrants tended to huddle together in one or two suburbs: they wanted to be close to the handful of shops that sold the food they needed. How did Arun's mother manage, in distant Canberra, to make those amazing curries? I asked him the other day. Arun's memory: 'There were a small number of Chinese shops in Dixon Street [in Sydney] which had some suitable ingredients, but to make the curries you had at our house, my mother used curry powder that was made in Sri Lanka, vacuum-sealed in tins and brought back in bulk whenever they visited home.'

He remembers the times when he came to our house for a meal: 'In fairness, your dad did a reasonable job, though, yes, it was chops and potatoes.' The real problem, he said, came when his family was invited to dinner by an Anglo friend and the host decided to treat the Sri Lankans to a taste of home, via curry made with Keen's curry powder, and often – he remembers – featuring sausages.

Australia had welcomed a flood of fresh talents and fresh tastes, but the new arrivals were largely invisible to the rest of the culture. It had been that way for some time. In her book *Lily on the Dustbin*, the Australian writer Nancy Keesing tells the story of a friend who worked as a travelling salesman in the 1930s, visiting country towns. On arrival in each town, he'd visit the local Greek café, saying to the owner: 'I'd like to eat in your café, but I don't want steak and eggs.' He'd ask if he could just have whatever the family themselves were eating that night, adding, 'I'll pay whatever you think is fair.' Keesing says her friend dined magnificently all over New South Wales, usually invited into the family dwelling above or behind the café, 'an honoured guest at a banquet that, with immense pleasure, his new friends had worked most of the day to prepare'. The café owners would explain that when they first arrived in town, they'd tentatively introduced a few Greek dishes on their menus, but these were met with distrust or even derision. Why eat anything else, when you could have steak and eggs?

*

After I'd completed my father's thorough three-recipe cooking course, I set out for my new home, a group house in Canberra. Two weeks later, I realised my diet consisted of nothing but steak, eggs and Worcestershire sauce. Alarmed that death might be imminent, I acquired a copy of *The Vegetarian Epicure* – a book that featured a hundred recipes in which one would take some form of vegetable matter and then dump half a ton of cheese on it. With particularly unpalatable veggies, more complex recipes were required, in which you would make sure the vegetable was completely dead by also drowning the bastard in sour cream.

As the years went on, things became ever more stylish. I particularly remember the Great Cooking-at-the-Table boom of 1977, in which butane burners were placed on the table top. All manner of Cointreau-infused crepes and buttery browned bananas were prepared, much to the delight of everyone –

normally with Cat Stevens's *Tea for the Tillerman* playing on a stereo nearby. There was also a great fondness for forcing the food to wear some sort of disguise. In most '70s kitchens, the phrase 'My chicken looks like chicken' would cause untold heartbreak. As a result, a lemon might be given toothpick legs, plus eyes and ears made of cloves, so that it resembled a fat piglet. A boiled egg might be served upright with a halved-tomato on top, as if it were a plump white man wearing a red hat. Cheese might be formed into the shape of a tree. It was like a witness protection scheme for food. The principle seemed to be: 'No way do we want people to recognise what they are eating.'

The aim, by and large, was to handle the food as much as possible: why serve olives in a bowl when you could instead pierce them with toothpicks then mount them on an orange in order to replicate the quills of a rather camp echidna? Notably, many 1970s recipes contained the word 'surprise' in the title. Who could be sure of the precise nature of the 'surprise'? The *Miss Australia Cookbook*, published in 1971, contains dinner-party recipes provided by winners of the Miss Australia competition. For example: 'Emerald Surprise' – a recipe that involves three rashers of bacon thrown together with a packet of frozen peas and a half pint of sour cream. Presumably the 'surprise' comes when all your guests make a sudden dash for the door.

People also loved logs and loafs – terrines full of gelatine or mayonnaise, or preferably both, often decorated with sliced eggs on top. There was a boiled-down horse in every meal. Then, of course, came the fondue, a dish that offered a chance to really get to know your neighbours, in particular, the germs they harboured within their gastrointestinal tract. Get any viscous substance – cheese or chocolate would do – heat it to the right temperature for bacterial growth, then invite everyone you know to dip and dip again.

Some of the best recipes of the decade have been collected in a book called *70s Dinner Party* by Anna Pallai. I particularly recommend the Tidbit Tree in which gherkins, cheese and pieces of pressed meat are served dangling from a plastic model of an old English oak . Or the chicken dressed up as if it were wearing a waistcoat made of bacon. Or the eggs halved and dressed as mice with radish ears.

Flipping through the recipes, certain patterns can be detected:

- If it's possible to use mayonnaise, go ahead.
- Now, add some more.
- Symmetry is very important. If serving a piece of, say, turkey, why not line up 12 prawns in neat rows on either side of the plate? Then line up some sliced olives and segmented oranges.
- Put a face on it. Okay, it's a pie, but why doesn't it have a face? How about two olives as eyes, a gherkin as a nose, maybe some parsley as the hair? Remember: all

your aesthetic choices should resemble those of a seven-year-old child with time on their hands.

Of course, every golden period must come to an end. People stopped using their chest freezers after a spate of power outages resulted in their having to eat a whole cow over a couple of sittings – a task that could really do in one's supplies of Worcestershire sauce. And the Cooking-at-the-Table boom ended after some very nasty incidents involving Nylon body-shirts, ruffled chest hair and butane burners. Last to go was the moulded gelatinous fish dish, made in the shape of a fish. Someone – history has lost the name – came up with the idea that instead of dismembering the fish, chopping it up, adding sour cream and powdered gelatine, then moulding it all back into the shape of a fish, you could try just serving the fish.

And so the '80s were born.

*

Maybe I'm being too negative. Many of the ingredients of the '70s were basically superfoods. Some examples:

The Sunny Boy
A triangular block of sweetened ice imprisoned in a waxed cardboard packet. The waxed paper could only be

loosened by tearing into the thing with your teeth, thus strengthening your teeth against the sugar that was about to flood your mouth: a near perfect meeting of contents and packaging.

The Musk Stick

You might think that pink is a colour rather than a taste, but the musk stick proves you wrong. The only way to describe what it tasted like is: 'Um, pink.' Importantly, the musk stick was designed with safety grooves so it would never slip out of your hand – presumably a reaction to the high number of lolly-related accidents in '70s Australia.

The Old 'Can Do' Attitude

By which was meant a can will do. Witness this genuine '70s recipe: take a chicken, and add 1 can of cream-of-mushroom soup, 1 can of cream-of-celery soup, and 1 can of cream-of-chicken soup. Plus some milk and what is described as '1 small onion'. What that actual vegetable is doing in there is anybody's guess.

Recipes Involving Brand-Name Products

In the 1970s, any company marketing a product that was vaguely edible offered a free recipe book in which the product in question was smuggled into every possible dish. Things were done with canned meat that were never meant to be done with canned meat. Edgell peas turned up in the most unexpected places. Take the example of the *Arnott's Crinkle Cut Potato Chip Recipe Book*, with its Spicy Meat Ring, as advertised in the *Australian Women's Weekly* of 18 March 1970. I know you'll want the recipe:

Spicy Meat Ring
Ingredients: *2 lb mince, 2 cups Arnott's Barbecue-flavoured Chips, Small onion, Horseradish cream, 2 eggs.*
Method: Combine. Pack into a greased 10-inch ring tin. Bake for 45 minutes. Turn out onto serving platter. Fill centre with heated Arnott's Crinkle Cuts.

As the booklet puts it: 'A taste-tempting dish'.

Home-Delivered Soft Drink
Soft drink may not immediately suggest itself as a superfood but consider this: only one family in each street had the stuff delivered. All the other children sat on their front steps contemplating their own tightwad parents, watching as the truck went by, the colourful bottles tinkling together in their wooden crates, clanking its way towards the spoilt O'Shaughnessy kids at number 18. At that point, a steely determination entered our

hearts: we would work hard and study hard – anything to build a life that would allow us to leave our awful parents and subscribe, via our own funds, to this most excellent service. Thus, did one superfood breed ambition in a million suburban kids.

Cheese and Crackers

Is there any more perfect or sophisticated combination? First off, there is the Jatz cracker, also featuring safety-grip edging, perfectly sized to be grasped between thumb and forefinger. Then the cheddar cheese, cubed. Still doubt it's a superfood? You may not have noticed the slice of gherkin, rich in Vitamin C.

Wagon Wheels

Okay, sure, I take your point: Wagon Wheels were full of sugar and salt and the marshmallow goo tasted like industrial waste. Consider, though, its role as a *psychological* superfood. However unhappy your childhood, however much you felt these were years to be endured on the way to adulthood, you can at least hold a Wagon Wheel today and think: 'You know what, they used to be bigger.' The inescapable conclusion: your childhood may have contained more sunshine than you remember.

Lamb Chops with Lots of Fat

Do you have a problem with snacking? Standing, late at night, bathed by the light of the open refrigerator door, rooting around for what can only be described as 'dessert-dessert' – the titbit to follow the earlier titbit which followed dinner. Some say you are an undisciplined greedy guts. I say you are not eating enough main course. The answer is a serve of that '70s superfood known as 'Tuesday night dinner'. This comprised three lamb chops with giant fatty tails, a pile of buttery Deb mashed potato as big as your head and a small serve of beans that had been boiled for three hours. Get through that lot and you'll be nailed, groaning to the couch, unable to even think about dessert for weeks. Yet again: problem solved.

French Onion Dip

The recipe is simple: take a bucket of sour cream and throw in a sachet of French Onion Soup Mix. Add some chopped hard-boiled egg if you want to impress. The mystery – with which science still struggles – is how food this high in calories produced a population in which obesity was so rare. The answer, of course, was that the French onion dip tasted so repulsive that the bowl was left untouched until the end of the night, at which point people would use it to extinguish their cigarettes. It remains perhaps the ultimate low-calorie entertaining option: one in which no calories at all were consumed.

Free School Milk

Ever wonder why a previous generation of Australians was protected from nut allergies and asthma? The answer is free school milk, supplied to all schoolchildren from 1951 to 1973. By delivering it to the school at 7 a.m. and then leaving it in the full sun for the four hours until 'little lunch', thus to curdle and incubate a thousand strains of bacteria, the government created a drink that was fatal to all but the strong. It was a eugenics scheme written in dairy. If you made it through kindergarten alive, you'd never again have a day's sickness.

Free school milk: a eugenics scheme written in dairy.

*

Here's one final observation about the stodgy nature of 1970s cooking, of the endless white bread and processed cheese, and the limitless supply of meat and potatoes. It appears to have had an alarming effect on the nation's guts. Flip through the magazines of the time and one thing is clear: the whole nation was badly bunged up. Every meal, to borrow a phrase from David Sedaris, was like packing a musket. The pages of the *Australian Women's Weekly* are ablaze with cures for constipation – a condition considered to be the cause of many of society's ills. For example, a misbehaving child: 'Irregularity could be the hidden devil in him,' says the advert for Laxettes. Dose him up and 'he'll be an angel in the morning'.

All ages are catered for. There's a chocolate-flavoured laxative for the kids – 'He'd rather be a regular guy'; then there's a rheumatoid arthritis treatment for the oldies with a 'gentle laxative effect'. Or perhaps you'd prefer DuoVac, the 'easy way to end constipation', even if the name does contain a somewhat alarming reference to vacuuming.

You can only imagine the relief when the 1980s started, some fibre was introduced to the evening meal, and the whole nation could retire to the bathroom and finally let rip.

CHAPTER FOUR

Car Trouble

Young Australians are no longer passionate about owning a car, so we are told. All the feelings that used to be associated with the purchase of your first vehicle – independence, sexual freedom, the ability to order pizza – are now connected with the purchase of your first phone. I wonder if, in three decades time, this generation will talk about their first phone with the same misty-eyed nostalgia that others reserve for memories of that first car? 'Ah, yes, mine was a Samsung SGH-A127 with 0.3-megapixel camera plus an inbuilt currency converter and world time,' one aging millennial will say, and his mates will laugh and wonder about the existence of a device so primitive. Then, like the car owners before them, they'll move onto the relationships that flourished thanks to that first purchase: 'And you know what?' one will say, wrapping his arm around his wife of 30 years. 'It was this lucky lady with whom I did my first sexting.'

Certainly in the 1970s the car was everything. That's why many people can recount every detail of their first vehicle. Mine was a Toyota Corona, purchased from my friend David at a cost of $500. He met me out the back of my father's newsagency, and I counted a stack of $20 notes into his hand, money hard-earned home-delivering newspapers in the freezing Canberra pre-dawn. It seemed the most important transaction of my life, signalling the arrival of adulthood.

Importantly, the car had bench seats – a crucial feature since, if you took the left-hand corners with sufficient force, your girlfriend might hopefully be propelled along the seat towards

My first car, bought for $500 from my friend David. I was ripped off.

you. Right-hand cornering was done more delicately, lest she take the chance to slide in the other direction. The Corona had numerous dents, no radio and no security, meaning you had to affix a cumbersome lock on the steering wheel each time you parked the thing. Talking about parking, the battery had long before stopped working so the only way to start the motor was by means of a clutch start. Most of my late adolescence was spent driving around trying to find a parking place on a hill, with a drive-way in front, so I could clutch-start my way towards actual motoring. Now I think about it, it's clear that David ripped me off. As soon as I finish writing this, I'm going to search for him on Facebook and demand my money back.

To be fair to David, in those days most cars didn't work. The boot of every vehicle was littered with plastic soft-drink bottles filled with water to replenish the radiator when it overheated. They were always slightly greasy, having rolled around in the boot for so long. Female drivers opted to wear pantyhose or stockings on any long journey; their hosiery crucial when replacing the broken fan belt. Many motorists carried eccentric repair kits, due to the ever-present likelihood of a breakdown. A potato cut in half and smeared on the windscreen was said to repel water, thus compensating for a broken windscreen wiper. Soap, some claimed, could be popped in the petrol tank to plug a leak. Others carried a dozen eggs: crack a couple into the radiator and they would coagulate over any holes or cracks.

Open anyone's boot and there was a virtual corner store of ingredients: in the absence of a breakdown, you could prepare a meal for five and then wash up afterwards.

I mentioned all this on radio one day, and Dave from Woy Woy rang to tell the story of how, as a young man in England, he was stopped by police while driving his precious Mini. The officers found a hammer in the boot and charged him with 'carrying an offensive weapon'. He tried to explain that such an implement was commonly carried by Mini drivers, but the coppers didn't believe him. The case went to court, where luckily Dave struck a judge who understood the realities of being the owner of a Mini.

> **Judge:** Why did you have a hammer in your car?
> **Dave:** I drive a Mini, your Honour.
> **Judge:** 'Starter motor?'
> **Dave:** Yes, Your Honour.
> **Judge:** Case dismissed. Enjoy your driving.

Apparently, a starter motor contains graphite brushes which can clump together, a fault particularly common in the Mini, and a gentle rap with a hammer was the oft-practised cure.

One of my main complaints about TV bio-pics with a '70s setting is the apparent reliability of the vehicles. In programs about Molly Meldrum, Paul Hogan or Ita Buttrose, characters are shown jumping into their vehicles and, soon after, are depicted arriving at their destination. Totally unlikely. In reality, no one ever arrived anywhere. A splash of rain was enough to bring many cars to a standstill. On particularly wet days, radio stations would have regular crosses with the local motoring association, so that listeners could be updated with the current waiting time for emergency assistance. The wait might be up to four hours, but most members were understanding. After all, it *was* raining.

You may think I was hopeless at mechanical matters, and therefore author of my own fate. More manly types, you may be observing to yourself, would have managed things better. Not true. I cite the Australian actor Shane Jacobson, a self-confessed car nut. In his book *Rev Head*, Shane recounts how, in one of his movies, he improvised a scene in which his truck wouldn't start: 'I poked my tongue to the left and turned the key again. It didn't start that time either, so I poked my tongue to the right with no more success. Finally, I stuck my tongue straight out and the engine sprang to life. The actor sitting beside me was mystified. Being a millennial, she had no idea. Cars just worked for her; there was no need in her life for praying, crossing fingers, rubbing dashboards, sticking out the tongue or having a good stern chat to a car just to get the thing to turn over.'

He's right about the tradition of discussing matters with your vehicle. A few decades back, everyone kept up a constant dialogue with their car – particularly when they were trying to get up hills. It was like riding a horse. 'Come on, you can do it.' 'Good boy.' 'That's the way.' On a steep hill you'd rock backwards and forwards in your seat to provide extra momentum. Most people would also give their car a name, so that it could be directly addressed. 'Well done, Betty, you know you are a real champion'.

Hills were always an issue. I had a friend whose car lost its rear wheel coming down Clyde Mountain, on the route from Canberra to the New South Wales South Coast; it simply detached on a sharp corner and bounced down the mountain. Most of the time, the problem was less dramatic: an overheated radiator. Those making the journey between Melbourne and Sydney would pause at Berrima and discuss their forthcoming assault on Razorback Mountain. Do you think the car will make it? Have you checked the oil? Are there two slightly greasy water bottles in the boot? The tone of voice was one normally reserved for the ascent of Everest. Yet there was good reason for such discussions at Base Camp Berrima: as the cars laboured up Razorback Mountain, a large proportion of vehicles would give up on life. On a typical Sunday afternoon, it would be like the Iraqi retreat from Kuwait: the roadside littered with smoking ruins.

By chance, I recently drove the same stretch of road and am forced to report that the staggeringly steep hill of my memory is actually a gentle incline, hardly perceptible from the horizontal. This proves the very crap nature of our cars.

Even the expensive ones didn't work. In fact, the more expensive the vehicle, the more likely it was to never start. At the same time as I bought the Toyota, my father splurged on a Triumph Stag, a vehicle so pricey it hardly ever reached the end of our street. The Stag was built in Britain and – to quote Wikipedia – 'rapidly acquired a reputation for mechanical unreliability, usually in the form of overheating'. My father took to sitting in the car while parked in the driveway, in the way a rich man might enjoy pottering around on his yacht, while berthed in the marina, without necessarily wanting to confront the dangers of the open sea. The Stag, however, did very well in safety ratings, probably because it was impossible to get the thing on the road.

As for my Toyota, the car lasted long enough to transport me on my first weekend away with my new love interest – Debra. It was 1979. We went to Wombeyan Caves, in the Southern Highlands of New South Wales, and I put up a tent, borrowed from a friend, my efforts illuminated by the headlights of the car. Alas, this soon drained the inadequate car battery, the lights fading, then flickering, then entirely disappearing, leaving me to complete the work in half-darkness as the inevitable high wind sprang up. When the construction was complete, I summoned Debra to the entrance with a flourish, much like a maître d' inviting a diner to their table in an upmarket restaurant.

'Your tent, Madame.'

Debra just stood there, arms folded, looking at the tent, which was now listing to one side and slumping in the middle.

'An inadequate erection,' she said grimly. 'No doubt the first of many.'

She did, however, join me in the tent. Our love story could not be derailed – even by the crap battery of a 1968 Toyota Corona.

*

I asked my friend Philip about the cars of his childhood in Tasmania. He had the same memories about mechanical breakdowns, recalling the way his mother would chant at his father every time they approached a hill: 'Don't let it boil!' and the big bag of tools his father kept in the boot for running repairs. He also remembered how, in suburban Launceston in the early '70s, a celebration would greet the arrival of any new car. 'The proud owner would park their new vehicle in the driveway and all the neighbours would come over and admire it. The adults would have a turn in the driver's seat, and there'd be much discussion of all the features. It was a rare and special event.'

It was a sunny tale, but then Phil's mood shifted. He recalled a darker story. 'People forget the carnage. There were no seatbelts; drink driving was common. The road toll was huge. Everyone knew someone who'd died, but it was just considered part of driving.' He told me about the night his parents were woken by someone forcefully knocking on the door. It was a policeman. The couple next door had been involved in an accident coming back from the golf club social. The car had run off the road and collided with a power pole. The father had been killed, the mother terribly injured. The police had somehow worked out that their 10-year-old son was still in the house, asleep.

'This,' said Phil, 'was before they had child welfare departments or social workers. The police did their best. They'd wake the neighbour.'

As it happened, Phil's father was a school principal, but this, Phil insisted, had nothing to do with the story. 'The police wouldn't have known Dad's profession; they just assumed that the neighbour would be familiar with the child.' He remembered his dad going next door, picking the sleeping boy from his bed, carrying him into their own spare room, and tucking him in. The next morning, it fell to Phil's father to wake the boy and break the news.

*

The Australian road toll peaked in 1970, when 3,798 people died. By 2017, the figure had fallen by about two-thirds – to 1,225 – despite a doubling in the population. In the 1970s, driver deaths were just seen as part of the cost of driving, an attitude reflected in the language we still use. Darren Chester, a one-time minister for transport and member for the Victorian seat of Gippsland, made the point after three of his young constituents were killed: 'I refuse to use the word "toll",' he told Parliament. 'A toll suggests it's a price we have to pay to use our roads.'

The changes came slowly. From 1969, it was mandatory for new vehicles to be fitted with front seatbelts, but it wasn't until 1972 that drivers around the country were required to wear them. A survey of Sydney drivers in 1970 found that as few as 15 per cent of drivers were using the belts that had been fitted; at that point, Victoria was the only state in which the belts had to be worn. The legislation also exempted children under eight years of age, partly because the politicians couldn't figure out how to fine people so young that they didn't have any money. A few years on, some genius worked out you could fine the driver instead, although how – in the interim – they planned to sting the nine-year-olds remains a mystery.

Officer: Okay, kid, hand over the Barbie.

Anyway, the upshot was that, through much of the '70s, kids would stand on the front bench seat of the car, like tiny rockets just waiting to be launched through the windscreen.

Safety restraints for children were introduced from 1976 onwards, depending on state legislation, with Victoria again leading the way. It was the same story with random breath testing – coming to Victoria in 1976, but not to Queensland and Western Australia until 1988.

Each of these changes was met with big opposition. Driver groups, such as the NRMA in New South Wales, opposed the compulsory fitting of seatbelts as 'an unnecessary restraint on individual freedom'. The NRMA also didn't object to a few drinks before driving: prior to 1968, there was no prescribed alcohol level. If a limit was to be imposed, said the NRMA, it should 0.08 milligrams per millilitre, no lower, and drivers should only be tested if police were acting on reasonable suspicion the driver was drunk. The organisation won on both scores: a prescribed alcohol level of 0.08 was introduced in New South Wales on 17 December 1968, with testing limited to those who'd excited suspicion.

The campaigns against roadside breath testing were intense. *The Australian* newspaper called it a gross intrusion on human rights. Queensland's minister for transport, Don Lane, also didn't think much of the idea: 'Random breath tests are a fascist or Nazi-style approach,' he said.

Despite the opposition, the impact of the introduction of roadside breath testing was immediate. In New South Wales, where it was introduced in 1982, there was a 48 per cent drop in fatal accidents in the first four and a half months. In that short period alone, the new law had prevented 194 deaths. It's a number that may give some idea of how many people were weaving around on the roads pissed out of their minds. When the 30th anniversary of the law was marked in 2012, the New South Wales roads minister, Duncan Gay, accurately and bravely described the culture around drink driving in the 1970s:

> I was one of those guys. I was more interested in going
> to rugby training for a couple of hours and going around
> the bar for a couple of more hours afterwards. There was
> a feeling in the community, if you had a couple of drinks,
> you could actually drive better than without it. We were
> stupid. We were absolutely stupid. If it wasn't for [the new
> laws] a lot of my friends and perhaps even myself wouldn't
> be here today.

In the '60s and '70s, the car and the freedom it brought were embraced with uncritical glee. Little wonder. Often it was the site of the first kiss, the two young humans squeezed together in the back seat, their over-excited breath creating their own foggy screen of privacy. How perfect that the fogginess rose in lock-step with the passion – a light mist for a chaste kiss, and a dense pea-souper for more serious excursions. Cars were fun – so much so they were allowed to remake the world in their own image. We stood by as they poisoned our lungs, chewed up our countryside, inspired foreign wars with the aim of securing fuel supplies, and required that freeways be bulldozed through our suburbs. It was as if we were unwilling to put any limit on a device so intriguing, so liberating. Adding a seatbelt took years. Lead was left in the petrol because the engine seemed to like it. And Ralph Nader – who thought it would be better if American cars stopped bursting into flames – was considered a dangerous radical.

*

A few years on from its role as a teenage love nest, the car would emerge in a new guise: the family wagon, home to squabbling children on long trips up and down the coast. I never went on these sorts of trips as a child, on account that I came from a weird family in which the two parents hated each other. But – having talked to friends – I feel I can offer a portrait of how things went down in this most rich of periods. The trip itself would start at 5.30am – 'Just so we can beat the traffic' – a decision shared with every other family, leading to a massive traffic jam 10 minutes from the end of your street. There followed a relentless drive up the coast, stopping for no one, sweaty bodies squirming on vinyl car seats, a wind-tunnel of hot air blowing through the open windows, every request for a toilet break angrily denied, as if life itself depended on arriving in Forster, Surfers Paradise or Sorrento by a reasonable hour.

Once you'd arrived in Forster, Surfers Paradise or Sorrento, there'd then be the matter of accommodation.

Some families would stay in the local caravan park. It was often in the best spot – right by the beach – but it afforded scant privacy. You'd book in at a small office/shop bristling with signs, each one hinting at some past drama. They'd say things like: 'Do Not Ask For Credit', or 'Do Not Ask to Borrow Our Electric Toaster', or the intriguing 'Do Not Allow Dogs to Urinate on Electrical Wires'. Nearly every establishment would feature a glass counter, with a large sign sticky-taped to the surface, saying 'If unattended, please ring bell, DO NOT TAP ON THE GLASS WITH A COIN!!!', the capital letters indicating the level of passion. Despite these prohibitions, aficionados claim that it was all worth it: if you happened to be 15 years of age, the caravan park offered the perfect opportunity to have an intense and fairly innocent love affair with somebody who would, by 26 January, be safely 200 kilometres away.

Some of those in the holiday park stayed in tents, the bumper bar of their car providing at least one anchorage point for the various tarps. Others stayed in onsite vans, often with extensive trelliswork giving them the appearance of a permanent dwelling. The majority, though, stayed in their own van, towed all the way from town, in heroic defiance of OPEC's attempts to push up the price of petrol. In fact, 1975 – two years on from the oil crisis of '73 – represented peak caravan. In that year alone, 12,000 caravans were produced by the Viscount company, the leader in a market that also included Ambassador, Franklin, Millard and Chesney.

Others – perhaps more middle class – would rent a house for the fortnight, sometimes sharing with best friends from the street they lived in back in the city. Why go somewhere new if you didn't know all the people once you got there? Such rental properties, as if by law, offered a stove in which at least two hot plates didn't work and three battered saucepans too small to cook anything. Plus there were four plastic wine tumblers, badly scratched, a broken banana lounge for which the renter would later get the blame, and a hot water supply immediately defeated by the teenage boy's first shower. There was also a locked cupboard. This was where the owner of the house kept all the good stuff. The renter was left asking the question: 'How can they rent a house this unpleasantly hot and not have any electric fans?' The renter would then supply themselves with the answer: 'Ah, that's right, the locked cupboard. Oh, oh, that I could get inside.'

Often the visitors would just gather together, staring at the padlock, imagining what was in there. Fans. Pasta pots. Banana lounges that were yet to be broken. A spare TV. It was, in the mind's eye of the renter, Ali Baba's Cave. You could almost imagine the owner was inside, cradling the goods like Gollum in Lord of the Rings, mumbling 'my precious, my precious'.

*

The third option was booking into the local motel. In the early 1970s these would have several consistent features:

- There would be a belligerent old guy behind the counter.
- The sign advertising the pool would be almost as big as the pool itself.
- The electric kettle would nearly, but not actually, fit under the tap in the tiny basin. You'd have to use your hand to, well, whoosh water into the spout.

There was also the toilet festooned with an Easter Show–style sash to celebrate the fact that, on this special occasion, they'd remembered to clean it. And the hot water never worked. (Come to think of it, it still doesn't.) Having a shower in your typical motel – the water going from burning hot to dead cold then back to burning hot – always sang a song of your fellow residents. 'Ah, ouch,' you said, as the lady in unit 3 turned off her shower and 'Ah, ouch', you said again, as the man in unit 12 started his. Then, just when the temperature had stabilised, there was the long period in which the man in unit 14 attempted to fill his kettle, constantly fiddling with the hot and cold as he tried to figure out why the motel had purchased a kettle that wouldn't fit under the tap.

Then there was breakfast. The breakfast menu had – still has – tick-boxes to indicate time of delivery, and more tick-boxes for the food. To be fair, your breakfast would normally arrive on time, slotted through the two-way hutch built into in the wall. Your selected meal would be on the tray, plus two slices of white, rubberised toast and a butter pat so hard that the polar ice-caps would melt before it softened. At this point, the customer might whinge about how shit everything was – the hot water, the breakfast and the strange stains on the bedspread – but in order to complain, you had to search the property looking for a staff member. This was not a good idea as, in the process, you'd come across cupboards filled with rows of enormous PVC buckets, apparently identical, yet variously labelled as 'Shampoo', 'Cooking Oil' and 'Pool Cleaner'. Next to them would be a handwritten poster stuck on the wall for the benefit of employees: 'The Blue One is Pool Cleaner NOT COOKING OIL'.

What did I say about signs that hinted at some past, tragic narrative?

Whatever your choice of accommodation – caravan park, house or motel – the next two weeks would be spent getting fiercely burnt, to the extent that you could no longer travel with comfort in the Kingswood as large parts of your flesh would become stuck to the vinyl upholstery whenever you tried to get out. Talk to nearly anyone about Australian life in the 1970s, and you'll encounter the word 'peeling'. There was no sunscreen. No rashies. No hats. The main summer occupation, particularly among young Australians, was shedding skin.

Then it would be time for the drive back home.

On the return journey, the father would be slightly more relaxed, having spent two weeks in a state of perpetual alcoholic stupor. Due to his expansive mood, he would insist that everyone partake in an educational detour, most commonly a trip to the state's Third Largest Tree, or Fifth Biggest Blow Hole, before driving 60 kilometres inland to have a beer in the Famous Wallydilldah Hotel. (Why didn't anyone mention it closed in 1969?) Alternatively, it could be a trip off the highway to see the town in which some bloke built a scale model of Florence out of local marble, now on display at the town hall, donations appreciated.

After one of these attractions, or maybe all of them, it was back in the car to complete the trip home – five hours in a traffic jam on the highway, sandwiched between multiple caravans, the rear-vision mirror blocked by li-los, Eskys and the children, who were busy with a rehearsal of World War III. A sample:

David (to his sister Susan): I'm going to lean over your side and breathe up all your air.

Susan: Mum, David is stealing my air.

Father: Quiet, both of you. I've had enough. If you don't stop fighting, I don't know what I'll do.

These words were being said simultaneously by a thousand parents in a thousand cars, the same phrase rising from the valleys and bouncing along the ridgetops, the giant shared sigh of an Australian highway. Suitably chastened, the children, all the children, would fall quiet, for as long as three or four seconds. Hostilities would then be resumed at an ever higher pitch. Within 10 minutes, the rear bench of the Kingswood – the rear bench of every Kingswood – would have taken on the appearance of the Korean Peninsula, the seat divided at the 38th parallel, with a heavily defended border, on either side of which complex military exercises were being performed. These variously comprised: children kicking each other, but in the footwell, where it couldn't be seen; children mounting border raids involving pinching and slapping; and constant verbal threats.

Susan (to her brother David): I'm going to lean over your side and steal your view.

David: Mum, Susan is stealing my view.

Father: Quiet, both of you. I've had enough. If you don't stop fighting, I don't know what I'll do.

Actually, he did know what to do: another educational stop. This time, it would be the small town with a local history museum. Inflicting an hour in a local history museum is as close as you can get to physically attacking your children without the social services being called. The museum would include every old jam jar that had been dug up within 90 kilometres of the place, plus a couple of ploughs so broken down they'd failed to sell at auction. Unless you were 97 years old, and actually owned the plough, the museum would induce a catatonic stupor so deep that the whole party became pacified ... right until you got back on the road. At which point:

> **Susan:** Mum, David's making noises with his bottom.
>
> **Mother:** David, don't make noises with your bottom.
>
> **David:** I'm not making sounds with my bottom. My bottom is making sounds with my bottom.
>
> **Father:** Quiet, all of you. I've had enough. If you don't stop fighting, I don't know what I'll do.

It's at this point that the car would break down.

Did I mention that, back in the '70s, the cars always broke down?

CHAPTER FIVE

The Wages of Sin

Australia has always had a liking for rules. In Queensland, for instance, it is still illegal to keep a pet rabbit. The penalties are severe: $44,000 and six months in prison. South of the border in New South Wales, you can have as many bunnies as you like. As recently as 2016, the confusion led to a confrontation between police and a family accused of keeping a pet rabbit in a caravan park south of Brisbane. When police arrived at the caravan, the owners tried to convince the officers that the rabbit was, in fact, a guinea pig. This did not fool the highly trained constabulary, who quickly noticed the 'guinea pig' in question had large floppy ears of the sort normally associated with a rabbit. The bunny, named Boo, was seized by the authorities then rehoused by a rabbit rescue charity. It now enjoys life south of the border in the welcoming town of Sawtell.

The story is interesting not only for the delightful sense of farce – 'No, really, his ears only go up like that when he's listening' – but for what it teaches us about Australia's love of legislation. We are, for instance, one of the few places in which you can be fined for leaving your car unlocked. Apparently, it's been proved that unlocked cars lead to an increase in crime. For instance: the crime that's just been committed by leaving your car unlocked.

So the national love of laws continues. It's nothing, though, compared to the way life was controlled in the 1960s and 1970s.

Censorship, for instance, was rigid. Through the 1960s, customs officers at the airport would consult the 'banned list' if they located any sort of book in a person's luggage. For much of the decade, the list included such literary efforts as D. H. Lawrence's *Lady Chatterley's Lover*, Brendan Behan's *Borstal Boy* and Vladimir Nabokov's *Lolita*. In the case of *Lady Chatterley*, the Australian ban was maintained even after the book had been cleared by the British courts. The prime minister of the time, Robert Menzies, told cabinet that he wouldn't want his wife, Dame Pattie, to read it. More bizarrely, a sombre legal account of the *Lady Chatterley* obscenity trial – held in London in 1960 – was also banned lest Australian readers cunningly reconstruct the book's narrative via the evidence presented.

Sometimes, it came down to the precise timing of your arrival. One Sydneysider, Alastair Wilson, recently recounted his experiences of arriving in Australia in March 1969, and being asked by customs if he was carrying any books. 'When I produced *The Ginger Man* by J.P. Donleavy, the officer took it away to check whether it was still on the banned list. He returned to tell me it had been removed the previous week. At that moment I wondered what kind of country I had paid my 10 quid to come to.'

The New Zealanders were ahead of us in some ways. While James Joyce's *Ulysses* was banned here, it was available across the ditch – causing a regular trade in smuggled copies. On the other hand, when the film of *Ulysses* came to New Zealand in 1967, the chief censor decided it could only be shown in sessions segregated by gender. In Wellington, men could see the film at the St James Cinema, while women-only sessions were held at the Regent. Perhaps, at the end of each screening, the now sex-crazed groups met somewhere in the middle. Alas, history is silent on the resulting melee.

In both Australia and New Zealand, artistic merit was no excuse. As late as 1973, the Victorian Vice Squad seized six posters of Michelangelo's 'David' from a Melbourne bookstore, considering them pornographic. That night on television, Graham Kennedy mocked the process, filling the set with statues of David, whose groin he eyed off while saying: 'What a fuss about something that's been hanging around for 500 years.' The posters were returned, although David's power to scandalise was undiminished. His groin was again in the news, a year or two later, after large plastic models were erected in a Melbourne department store. David's private parts were apparently bang on eye level when you came down the escalator. A discreet covering was added, much to the relief of shoppers.

To be fair, by the end of the 1960s the floodgates were starting to open. Despite the best efforts of the various branches of the Vice Squad, there was a rising tide of filth and nudity. As the sportscaster Rex Mossop put it, when making a citizen's arrest of an underdressed sunbather: 'I don't think the male genitals or the female genitals should be rammed down people's throats.'

There was a good side to this new freedom, at least as far as my father's business was concerned. Once the policy was softened, even a normal newsagency was suddenly able to stock material the likes of which the public had never seen. My father sold stacks of the stuff – the worst of it from a curtained-off alcove beneath the stairs, a trapezium of shame. As a young would-be progressive, I was embarrassed by my attendance at a private school – the toffy Canberra Grammar – but at least I knew the family secret: all the fees were paid for from my father's controversial selection of 'one-handed magazines'. After he died, I went through his papers and found a letter of complaint sent by one of his customers, the perfectly named Mrs Flora Beauchamp. In June 1974, Mrs Beauchamp described entering our newsagency for the purpose of selecting some stationery:

When casually glancing around for my requirements, my eye was arrested by a disgusting picture on some material for sale. The picture is a degradation of womanhood and an affront to common human decency ... I wonder the young ladies on your staff do not feel repulsion at handling such pollution – though I did notice they wore protective gloves.

Pinned to her letter was a carbon copy of my father's reply – a masterly example of evasion through robust agreement:

Dear Mrs Beauchamp,

Your recent letter came as a tonic, for I had come to the conclusion that the entire community had lost all sense of propriety. It is, as you suggest, within my authority to remove this material from the shelves – and I have pondered the question many times because I myself feel offended.

He went on this vein at some length, laying it on pretty thick, noting the 'quite outrageous pornographic material' that was suddenly available, before finally concluding that he had 'no authority to assume the role of judge on public morality'.

Phew! The school fees were safe.

It wasn't only the glossy magazines that were helping our profits. In late 1972, *The Little Red Schoolbook* was published by a local printer, thus avoiding an importation ban. It was an adaptation of a Danish manual, designed for schoolchildren, with frank advice about sexuality, drugs and – perhaps most shocking of all – how to rebel against the needless tyranny of one's teachers. I still have my copy from the time, which – if you throw it in the air – lands open on page 93: sex. Quite early in the chapter, it notes that females can achieve an orgasm, proof of the dangerous nature of the information within. My father ordered a large stack of *The Little Red Schoolbook*, which he put in various dump bins out the front of his store. As a conservative small businessman, I'm sure he didn't endorse the rebellious contents, but he certainly was willing to collect the $1.75 cover price. I remember various of my schoolfriends queuing up to buy it – sometimes when I was on the cash register. My father would interrupt the transaction, commenting in a somewhat desultory fashion, 'Well, as long as you think your parents would approve,' before rapidly ringing up the sale.

We schoolboys were not the only people talking about the book. When the cabinet papers for 1972 were released under the 30-year rule in 2003, the *Sydney Morning Herald* noted that '*The Little Red School Book* was only a little book, but cabinet spent a lot of time discussing it.' In fact, cabinet discussed the book on at least four occasions. Doug Anthony, then deputy prime minister, told his fellow ministers that the book was a handbook for juvenile revolution and anarchy – a publication whose subversive nature endangered society. The customs minister, Don Chipp, replied that he had no power to ban its importation as it was being printed locally – besides which, he wouldn't want to ban it even if he could. Chipp also lifted a ban on 'certain marital aids' after the Health Department had told him that they were not harmful and could be beneficial. No longer would women need to buy a 'back massager', only to find that other parts of the body were also holding an awful lot of tension.

It was not only The Land Before Avocado. It was also The Land Before Vibrators.

Outside the cabinet room, the DLP Senator Jack Kane provided the assessment that Chipp had played a major role in eroding the moral basis on which Australian society depended. My father may well have agreed. But at least he had the profits from 15 boxes of *The Little Red Schoolbook*.

*

By the early 1970s, Britain was happily supplying whole mountains of filth to Australia, led by the now legal *Lady Chatterley's Lover*. Australia, for its part, returned the favour – sending Richard Neville and his mates to London in order to establish a local version of the satirical, salacious magazine *Oz*. Some months later, Neville and two colleagues were duly tried for obscenity.

While Mrs Flora Beauchamp was entirely right in identifying the filth being sold by my father, others saw sex even when it wasn't there. At one point during the trial, Neville was quizzed about an illustration in which a boy held a rolled-up copy of *Oz* – the true meaning of which was instantly spotted by the judge, Michael Argyle.

Judge: In [the illustrated boy's] left hand, [there's] a rolled copy of your magazine *Oz*?

Neville: That's right.

Judge: In the same position as an erect penis would be if that was his penis?

Neville: Quite honestly, your Lordship, until you just pointed it out, I hadn't noticed it.

Judge: Oh really?

Neville: Absolutely. I had never thought of comparing holding the magazine with an erection.

Judge: Hadn't you?

Neville: No, I hadn't.

Judge: I see. Very well.

Sometimes, as Freud might have said, a magazine is just a magazine.

At the end of this farcical process, the *Oz* editors were sentenced: Neville to 15 months in jail, Jim Anderson to 12 months, and their youngest collaborator, Felix Dennis, to only nine months – because, in the words of the judge, 'You are younger than the other two and very much less intelligent.' Three months later, the Appeal Court quashed the convictions, saying the judge's summing-up had grossly misrepresented the defendants' case. Oh, and the 'unintelligent' Felix Dennis later became a pioneer of personal computing magazines, amassing a fortune of more than £500 million.

*

Sleaze was not the only focus of the Australian authorities. Policing alcohol consumption was their other passion. In both Victoria and South Australia, pubs closed at 6pm, right up until the late 1960s: the infamous six o'clock swill. Customers arrived

Liquor laws seemed to be expressly designed to encourage both binge drinking and drink driving.

after work, say at 5.30, and then had half an hour to purchase and consume as many drinks as possible. By five minutes to six, there'd often be a line five deep at the bar, people begging and shouting for the bartender to serve them in time. At one point, the Victorian secretary of the Liquor Trades Union, Mr J. Coull, seriously recommended that drinkers should be supplied with plastic bibs to better protect their shirt fronts. Melbourne's *Argus* newspaper supported the idea, with the additional suggestion that cotton bibs might prove more absorbent than plastic. In the meantime, publicans removed anything that might prevent customers getting to the bar: pool tables, dartboards, even tables and chairs, all fixtures and fittings were done away with. It was a culture of perpendicular drinking, usually followed by horizontal regret. Needless to say, nearly all Australian pubs featured tiled walls and tiled floors. It was a design choice that reflected more than an interest in Edwardian ceramics.

Adding to the fierce atmosphere, most drinking was done under the 'shout' system. The first of, say, five drinkers would purchase a round of drinks for the whole party, expecting his due reward when the favour was repeated by each man in turn. In the Australia of the time, murder, bestiality and kidnapping were all frowned upon, but dodging one's shout was the gravest crime of all. To avoid the shame, many parties purchased their entire supply of beers when they first entered the hotel. The result: a typical pub would be full of men standing with legs apart, guarding the five or six schooners lined up on the floor. Little wonder that the six o'clock swill attracted amazed overseas tourists, who would arrive to take photos of the frenzy.

In South Australia, they also banned barmaids. Here's the theory of the time. Authorities believed the presence of female bar staff increased the amount of drinking, with men drawn into pubs just to enjoy the sight of the barmaid. Temperance campaigners called them 'the seductive lures'. Get rid of the barmaid and you'd get rid of drunkenness. There was no sign that the ban worked, but that didn't stop it remaining until 1967.

In Victoria, they had a more nuanced idea: they banned the employment of *new* barmaids, limiting employment to those already in the industry. The idea, according to Keith Dunstan in his book *Wowsers*, was that as the barmaids grew older they would no longer be able to use their alluring powers to attract men into the pub. The drinking rate would fall with each passing year as the barmaids became less and less attractive. The idea was not only ungentlemanly – women, I don't need to tell you, only become more attractive as they age – it was also difficult to police. The barmaid certificates were soon traded on the open market, much like taxi licences, with the result that many 20-something barmaids had paperwork indicating they were 54 years old. Or 67 or 79. Locals joked they must have discovered the elixir of youth, presumably in the beer they served – an idea which could only suggest the ordering of another round.

Stranger still were the laws on 'bona fide travellers'. In most Australian states, you could order a drink on a Sunday – but only if you could prove you were from out of town. The distance you were required to travel varied. In South Australia in the 1880s, it was five miles; in Victoria it was 10 miles in a direct line, but it had to be travelled on the day on which the alcohol was consumed. In New South Wales, right up until 1979, it was 30 miles – with the publican required to take a note of your 'reasons for travel' – typically transcribing your excuse into a large book, which would be kept on the bar. As a result, rural roads were full of groups of half-pissed men motoring from one town to another, all in the hope of a drink.

Instead of banning drink driving, the law made it mandatory.

*

Australia has always had a peculiar attitude to alcohol. The Australian wine and beer industries were developed with the aim of limiting alcohol abuse. You may see the flaw in this logic but, at the time, no one else did. In early Sydney, the real villain was rum (a hold-all term for any hard liquor), and if you could just replace the spirits with something lighter, all would be calm and peaceful: that was the belief. As a result, the first Australian brewery opened in Parramatta on 16 September 1804 – all funds provided by the colonial administration with the aim of flooding the colony with so much beer that people would become sober. When this didn't work out, extensive vineyards were planted with the same lofty ambition.

Some 200 years on, the expected outbreak of sobriety has yet to occur, but you never know.

Why, you may ask, were the early colonials so worried about rum? The problem was that it had effectively become the local currency. People were paid in rum, and so it was used to purchase goods. The government concluded this was a bad idea. For a start, it was hard to convince people not to drink their change. It could also create an existential crisis for customers who were in a tavern and trying to buy rum.

I'd like a quart of rum, please.
—Certainly, sir. That will cost you a quart of rum.

By the 1970s, despite the best efforts of the authorities, Australia was swimming in grog. Among the significant breakthroughs was the invention of the wine cask. It was first developed by Angoves in 1965, but it was the addition of a convenient tap – devised by David Wynn in 1971 – that led to its speedy domination of the wine trade. It's true that Australians also invented refrigeration, penicillin and the bionic ear, but nothing really compared to the invention of the wine cask. Among its features:

- The collapsible internal bag kept the wine from oxidising even once it had been opened.
- The emptied bag could be reinflated to serve as either a pillow – if one had consumed too much; or a silver disco ball – if one had consumed just the right amount.
- With a wine cask, no-one quite knew how much you were drinking.

Of all those features, it was the third that was by far the most popular.

Thus equipped, the '70s was Australia's booziest decade, at least since colonial times. My father, who considered himself a sophisticate, drank endless supplies of Mateus Rosé – a sweet Portuguese plonk which owed its popularity to its unusually-shaped bottle. It was, to quote the sales pitch of the time, 'The enchanting pink wine with the gentle suggestion of sparkle'. Dad's nightly bottle of Mateus would then be topped up with large drafts of gin, supplied from the 'bar' in the lounge room, another feature of the time. Others went for Australian wines, which were suddenly being advertised with catchy new names like Porphyry Pearl, Pineapple Pearl, Cold Duck, April Gold, Mardi Gras and, perhaps most famously, the locally made Asti Spumante, the name of which was said to quite accurately describe the effect.

As 15-year-olds, we preferred the swagger of vodka, swallowed direct from a hipflask, telling ourselves that it was the one drink that was odourless and thus undetectable by parents. This, of course, is one of the great teenage myths. Not only can you smell vodka on a person's breath, but even the most inattentive 1970s parent might wonder why their offspring, quite sprightly earlier in the evening, suddenly appeared to have trouble walking.

Certainly, among all generations, getting smashed was a popular response to the 1970s. From the early 1960s onwards, alcohol consumption rose steadily – finally peaking at 13.1 litres of pure alcohol in 1974–75 – a rate of consumption not matched at any time since the 1830s. The figure was equivalent to 2.9 standard drinks per person per day for everybody 15 or older. It's since dropped by about a quarter. Despite the media-led panic, young people today drink far less than those of us who grew up in the 1970s. They also take fewer drugs. I know no-one believes this, but here's criminologist Garner Clancey, quoted in *The Australian*: 'The National Health Drug Survey points to reduced drug and alcohol use across the board by young people. Lots of young people are using less alcohol, cannabis and a variety of other drugs and that's being matched by some research that talks about young people being less risk-taking today.'

*

During my youth, most of that sea of alcohol was consumed in the form of beer, but at least some came in the form of cocktails which – inexplicably – usually involved dairy products. As a young student at the Australian National University, I worked as a function waiter. I'd serve drinks at ANU Refectory, at events often involving 400 or 500 guests. The moment of terror arrived with the first order for a Fluffy Duck or Brandy Alexander. I'd request the drink from the barman and deliver it, knowing that half the women in the room would be simultaneously turning to their partner: 'Could I have one of those?' Later that night, I'd do the washing up and realise how hard it is to remove dried cream from 200 glasses. The men, meanwhile, would be combining the dregs of the white wine carafes with the dregs of the red wine carafes to create a brew we called ANU Rosé. Quite often, there were a few cigarette butts in there as well, but none of that worried the committed drinkers of the time.

*

Speaking of cigarettes, there was one exception to Australia's eagerness to police the world of sin. It was perfectly okay to smoke your head off. Smoking was allowed everywhere – in cinemas, buses, planes, offices, even in hospital wards and elevators. On domestic flights, it wasn't banned until December 1987. Up until then, there was smoking at the back of the plane, no smoking

Keystone Pictures USA / Alamy Stock Photo

There was outrage when smoking was banned on buses. At least the driver was still allowed to puff away.

at the front, and some very miserable people in the middle. Row 37, most of the time, was smoking – but not intentionally.

In pubs people were still smoking until at least 1998, at which point the law began to tighten – different states and territories acting with varied senses of urgency.

Even on buses and trains, smoking wasn't outlawed in most states until the mid-1970s. In New South Wales, for example, it was banned on suburban public transport by the relevant minister, Peter Cox, in 1977. The tobacco industry magazine, *The Australian Retail Tobacconist*, was unimpressed:

The ban on smoking on NSW Government trains, buses
and ferries has been called a Big Brother edict designed
to further harass the State's smokers … Many people,
smokers and non-smokers alike, have called the ban a
dictatorial act by Mr Cox.

The *Sydney Morning Herald* agreed – saying it was difficult to find
a case to support the ban. *Daily Mirror* columnist Jack Darmody
went further – saying the 1977 ban was an act of discrimination
against the working people who used public transport: 'The
good minister has the availability of a State Government car
to take him to and from his office. He doesn't even drive the
car himself. All he has to do is sit back and contentedly puff his
head off.' The paper noted that there was a further indignity for
the travelling smoker. Under the legislation, the bus drivers and
inspectors would still be allowed to smoke.

After all, it was their workplace.

There was also a whole language of smoking – words which
only now are starting to disappear from the lexicon. Oh, for a
donkey root while igniting an OPC. Or for a durry, a coffin
nail or even a cancer stick. Or for the moment in which two
rollies ('Has anyone got the makings?') are swapped for a tailor.

Perhaps I should provide a glossary? A 'donkey root'
involved lighting one's own cigarette using the burning end of
your friend's ciggy – the two phallic symbols, pressed end to

end, reminiscent, it was assumed, of the sex life of the male donkey. An OPC? That meant other person's cigarette, which could be requested using the mandated phrase: 'Can I bludge a fag?' It was, by and large, easier to bludge a rollie (a roll-your-own cigarette, using Tally-Ho papers) than a tailor-made – a commercially manufactured cigarette.

It seemed that everyone smoked. Bend down to pat a dog, and it would smell of second-hand fumes. So would any humans who'd spent time in either a workplace or on public transport. If your parents held a party, it was common for you to be enlisted to walk around offering to light people's cigarettes. The accoutrements of the smoking habit were a key part of the decoration of many a lounge room. There would be various large glass ashtrays together with an over-sized bowl containing booklets of matches souvenired from Gold Coast motels. (So ubiquitous were motel matches that the plot of most episodes of TV detective shows hinged on the discovery of a crumpled matchbook from a Coolangatta motel with a woman's phone number written on the inside flap.) There would also be a large table lighter fashioned from a piece of marble – so large that smaller children needed to use two hands to carry it around the room when offering a light.

Such children, aged perhaps eight or nine, didn't smoke themselves. Instead, they would buy pretend cigarettes. There were chocolate cigarettes – thin cigarette-like cylinders of

State Library of Victoria H2012.194/494

Bludging an OPC: In an attempt to fit in, it was wise to start early.

chocolate wrapped in Tally-Ho-style paper – with a panel of shiny foil representing the filter; or, alternatively an Australian-made product called FAGS – a kind of trainer-wheel cigarette featuring a stick of white confectionery with some red dye to simulate the burning end. FAGS, by the way, lasted all the way up to the 1990s, when the product was renamed FADS and the glowing red end was discontinued.

Back in the late 1960s, the same corner store that offered the FAGS would also happily sell you the real thing. At our local corner store in Sydney, cigarettes were available in packs of 20 or – for younger smokers trying to eke out their pocket money – in packets of 10. If that was too pricey, the owner sold individual cigarettes to child customers – fishing one out of a packet beneath the cash register on request. I can't remember how much they cost. Probably the same price as a musk stick.

From the early 1970s, anti-smoking advertisements started to appear – with messages that tended towards the straightforward. In the *Australian Women's Weekly* of 27 September 1972, for instance, there was a large photo of a teenage girl under the headline, 'PLEASE DO NOT SMOKE'. Denting the impact just a little was an advertisement on the facing page for a product called TarGard – a disposable filter. The text revealed that TarGard was 'the most important advance in protective smoking ever developed'. At 53 cents for a pack of five, said the ad, it was 'cheap insurance' for those who wanted to ignore the health campaigns and keep puffing. It had a competing bold headline: 'For people who would rather smoke than QUIT!'

Quitting, it seems, was for quitters.

Certainly, the industry was eager to fight back. Simon Chapman, now Emeritus Professor of Public Health at the University of Sydney, has studied the industry magazines of the time, such as the *Tobacco Trade Journal* of Queensland and Victoria's *Tobacco Journal*. Among their advice:

- Retailers should target teenagers: '... the teenage market is the adult market of tomorrow.' (*Tobacco Journal*, Victoria, 1964)
- Retailers should try to get people to buy in bulk: '"It looks like being a stormy weekend," you might well say to your customer, adding quietly, "have you made certain that you've enough smokes to see you through?".' (*Tobacco Trade Journal*, Queensland, 1971)
- 'Why not satirise the health warnings over cigarettes? You could say, for instance: "Do horses smoke? Yet horses have been found to suffer the lung disease emphysema, for which some health authorities blame cigarettes."' (*Tobacco Journal*, Victoria, 1969.)

After smoking all day, the nation spent the night coughing its guts out. Flipping through magazines and newspapers from the time, cough medicines – unsurprisingly – are regularly advertised. You might choose the Lixadil 8-Hour Cough Elixir for 'night-time coughing'; the Nyal Decongestant Cough Elixir for 'positive relief from persistent coughing', or – for the strong Australian male – Vick's Formula 44 Cough Syrup: 'It's a tough taste to take. But brace yourself.'

*

Despite puffing away almost constantly, not all my smoking memories are good. At school, there was an ocker science teacher who had doubts about my masculinity. He considered me effeminate and would roll his eyes whenever I spoke. With all the impressive logic of a 14-year-old, I worked out a solution to this problem. I was, after all, a smoker, and if he could just see me in action he would recognise my underlying masculine swagger. And so, when I next saw him at the local shops, I leaned out of the alcove in which I was puffing away so that he might spot me in my manly pursuit. He'd stop teasing me now!

Is that the most pathetic story you've ever heard? I think it may be. Of course, he just rolled his eyes in his customary way, marking me as not only effeminate but also stupid. Not only that, he reported me to the principal and I was duly flogged the next morning.

Even this didn't put me off smoking. For a start, the packet was a fashion accessory. My girlfriend of the time, Jane, would wear her packet of Alpine 'Menthol Fresh' in the back pocket of her jeans, stretching the already taut material just that extra bit tighter. The effect, when viewed from behind, always caused me to experience a sudden tightness of breath, which, admittedly, could have been the result of my own heavy smoking. Boys chose a pack of Winfield Blues, tucked under the right-hand sleeve of the T-shirt, believing it emphasised the chunky arm muscle we imagined lay beneath. Personality was often expressed though one's choice of cigarette – a factor which, in extreme cases such as my own, led to quite ludicrous outcomes, such as the consumption of a black Sobranie or an unfiltered Gauloise, proof that pretension can come in a packet of 20.

Later, when I settled down and children loomed, I pledged to give up and told Debra I'd been successful. I then kept smoking secretly while I was at work. God knows why she wasn't repelled by the odour. Presumably, she just thought I smelt like that. In those days, the *Sydney Morning Herald* held an annual Christmas party, at which skits were performed by the staff. I came unstuck when a young cadet performed a sketch in which I was bellowing angrily into a telephone, while chain-smoking. Debra, who was in attendance, was unsurprised by the rendition of me as a bad-tempered madman but, as we left, posed the tight-lipped question: 'Why, may I inquire, was the bad-tempered madman depicted as a smoker?'

The thrashing I received, while verbal rather than physical, had a remarkably similar quality to my run-in with the ocker science teacher. Which is to say, it didn't put me off smoking. More clandestine years followed, in which I felt like a hunted outlaw. A friend in a similar situation even went to the lengths of planting an aromatic gum tree near his back door. He and I would sneak out to the garage to smoke while our partners were inside, breaking off a leaf or two to chew before we made our way back into the house. His addiction may have been even more intense than my own. The poor tree was almost stripped bare.

In the end, I became so sick of the cycle – giving up smoking, resuming smoking, hating myself, giving up once more, and so on and on and on – well, in the end I just sighed with what little breath I had left, and gave up for good. Many others were going through the same process. In 1974, 37.5 per cent of Australian adults smoked. These days, it's about 13 per cent.

Whether it was the clothes or the attitudes, the smoking or the dodgy cars, the baggage of the 1970s took some effort to lose.

CHAPTER SIX

Making Our Own Fun

We made our own fun in the period 1965 to 1975. Much of it involved the burning of rubbish. In fact, burning your own rubbish was the main source of entertainment in Australia until well into the 1980s. The PlayStation hadn't been invented, Google didn't exist and sex was a just rumour from America, yet to be proven. So incineration – usually done in a 44-gallon drum up near your back fence – had to take up the slack. Most families would stick at it throughout the weekend, as a result of which the suburbs were always full of smoke. The Australian poet Bruce Dawe, in a work from 1969, described a householder he called *Homo suburbiensis*: 'He stands there, lost in a green confusion, smelling the smoke of somebody's rubbish.'

Incineration would begin first thing on Saturday morning, the children gathering, their small, entranced faces illuminated by the glow provided by the remnants of Friday night's fish

A home entertainment system, circa 1970.

supper. Saturday afternoon would yield the chance to burn boxes, newspapers and garden waste. By Sunday morning, the father of the household would be incinerating anything he could lay his hands on – chop bones, piano stools, the children's 'Explorers of Australia' project. The whole family would then rake any fallen leaves into a pile in the front gutter, before approaching with a match.

By Sunday afternoon, having exhausted the supplies of anything vaguely flammable, Dad would then suggest a trip to the tip, much to the enthusiasm of everyone. Once there, all the members of the family would clamber through fly-blown hillocks of stinking refuse and occasional spills of DDT and count themselves lucky. It was quite usual to return from the tip with more rubbish than you'd taken. In the words of the Colin Buchanan song, 'Frank the Scab': 'He'd take the half-full garbo down the road and come back with a grin and a trailer load.'

Generally, people were very interested in rubbish. Most homes were furnished with two tin bins, both of which were battered and bent, as if rejects from a Jamaican steel-drum ensemble. Each was equipped with a lid that, due to the battering and bending, didn't fit. There were no plastic bags for rubbish. You'd wrap your waste in sheets from the local paper – 'Not the Molnar cartoon, I want to keep that,' – and whack it in one of the bins. On garbage night the bins would be carried out to the roadside, where next morning they'd be heaved onto the shoulders of blue-singletted garbos who'd be rewarded at Christmas for this weekly show of strength by the provision of two longnecks of beer. Having emptied your bins, they would throw them back on the pavement with a tremendous life-affirming clatter, adding a new dent, before Frisbee-ing the lids in the general direction of your front door. If they hadn't woken everyone up for 52 consecutive weeks, they might have been given more than two longnecks of beer. Still, the service was excellent: all that rubbish gone in a flash. No wonder the Australian population voted for the Liberal Party for close to 200 years. The garbage service was *that* good.

*

It would be wrong to say that garbage disposal was the only source of entertainment. There was also the possibility of an occasional trip to the municipal swimming pool. This involved a rectangular prism of water so laden with chlorine that your eyes would turn red while still airborne in the act of diving in. Meanwhile, the showering area was so impregnated with tinea that you could lose a leg just by walking past. Kids peed in the pool, that's true, but only because they weren't game to take their chances with the weird old paedophiles in the change room. Also: no one used sunscreen. Teenagers would lie around smoking and sunbathing as if conducting a competition between the various forms of cancer as to which would prove the more virulent. You half-expected a race call: 'Skin is well positioned, but lung is gaining ground on the outside ...'

The whole watery circus was presided over by a bull-necked manager armed with a whistle and a deep hatred of children. In my case, he played a particular role, but more of that later.

I don't want to claim that everything was bad. There was some shade – but only from the sign that listed the banned activities. Running was forbidden. So was diving, splashing, singing, laughing or entering the pool if you'd recently visited the change rooms and thus lost a leg to tinea. There was also a kiosk, but the electrical supply to the fridge was so dodgy all the ice-creams became a slumped mass of ice crystals with a stick in the side. The pies, meanwhile, sat in a device optimistically named a pie-warmer. The dial was turned to the mark halfway between 0 (cold) and 10 (hot), a point that should have been marked: 'botulism'. In case the pies remained botulism-free, tomato sauce would be added via a plastic squeezer, pushed under the skin of the pie much like a doctor inserting a needle. If done correctly, the funnel would, over time, become encrusted with old sauce and bits of other people's pies, the lot then left in the sun to fester. Admittedly, this did give the pie a unique flavour I've missed ever since.

On my first visit to the local council pool, at age 10, I had the pie and sauce and avoided the paedophiles by weeing in the pool. Hopefully they hadn't got around to adding the dye. That was when I approached the concrete diving tower, the only entertainment device provided. The tower was built by evil council engineers to look squat and short while in fact being unfeasibly tall. I climbed up the first flight of stairs – 'Gee, there seem a lot of them' – and then around the corner – 'Oh, another whole flight' – before emerging on top, shuffling to the edge and looking down. Next thought: 'Oh my God, I'm too young to die.' By this time, a number of older boys, men, women and, just for humiliation value, seven-year-old girls had formed a queue behind me. There was no means of retreat.

At this point, the pool manager bellowed from below: 'Come on boy, jump.' I stood on the edge, mind disconnected from body, the roar of humiliation doing battle with simple fear, my small body swaying one way then the other as if buffeted by these forces, until humiliation grew so great that fear was pushed to one side. I dived, heading straight down, my arms stretched ahead as if my young body were a sleek missile that would soon pierce the water, splash-less, noiseless. Well, that was the idea. The trip downwards instead appeared to take some time, time in which I became slowly aware that my body was no longer heading straight down, that my arms had crunched up, my knees now bending, my legs now cycling in the air as if riding an imaginary bicycle, my body starting to flatten out, horizontal now, a falling ironing board, the water surface, grey like steel, heading up to greet me …

Somehow I heard the sound before I felt the pain, the immense noise of what was known as a bellyflop. Even the pool manager looked up. When I eventually surfaced, the sound was still echoing around the pool, having bounced off the banned activities sign. Afterwards, I floated feebly to the edge like a dead mackerel. Walking or breathing proved impossible for some time. Good outcome: the teenagers stopped smoking for a moment so they could stand up, point and laugh.

*

There was also watching television, such as it was. Memory is a strange thing. It selects the best and forgets the rest. If you think about '70s television, you may recall a series of highlights – *Certain Women*, *Callan*, *The Norman Gunston Show*, maybe even *Number 96*. But it also meant *Homicide*, a cop show that mainly consisted of detectives slamming the doors as they exited a recent model Ford; and *Skippy the Bush Kangaroo*, in which a marsupial from the family Macropodidae was able to give complex instructions via a series of *tsk-tsk* sound effects.

> *What's that, Skippy? Some criminals are operating a tax minimisation and drug importation scheme down by the creek? And if we approach from the north we'll be able to safely photograph them and present the evidence to police? Thanks, Skip!*

To get a sense of the typical fare on offer, I spent a morning looking through the newspaper TV guides of the time. The first place I landed was Thursday 25 February 1971. The prime-time entertainment that night included *Matlock Police*, *Father Dear Father*, *TV Fight of the Week* (from South Sydney Leagues Club), *Me Mammy* and something called *Curry & Chips*. I had to look up the last two – *Me Mammy*, I discovered, was a British sit-com about a young Irishman whose Catholic mother interfered with his bachelor lifestyle, while *Curry & Chips* starred a blacked-up Spike Milligan as a Pakistani immigrant who went by the name of Kevin O'Grady. It was cancelled after one series after viewers – even in 1971 – labelled it appallingly racist.

You'll accuse me of choosing a particularly bad night, so let's flip ahead a year to Wednesday 2 February 1972. This time, the choice on commercial television was a quiz show called *Coles $6000 Question*, an American police procedural called *Adam-12*, and a telecast of a local beauty pageant, the *Miss Victoria Sportsgirl*. The ABC, meanwhile, was offering *Here Come the Brides*, an American comedy/western. More? Fast forward another year to Saturday 10 February 1973, where the choice was *Junior Moneymakers* with Philip Brady, 'Las Vegas ... Australian Style', which featured the 'live opening of Australia's first official gambling casino, situated at Wrest Point, Tasmania,' and *The Black & White Minstrel Show* – a British variety show in which the performers appeared in blackface, pretending to be African Americans.

Not only wasn't there much to watch on the TV, half the time you couldn't see it. Few people had an external antenna, and instead relied on a pair of 'rabbit ears', which would sit atop the set. Prior to watching a program, the two metal antennae would be scissored in various directions – up, down and across like the legs of a synchronised swimmer – in the hope of achieving a picture that didn't dissolve into a series of zig-zagging lines. Often the only solution was to recruit a child to stand beside the set, finger touching the antenna, for the duration of the program. If you wonder why so few Australians from this time managed to learn a second language, or win a Nobel Prize for Science, now you know the answer: most Australian childhoods were largely spent holding the antenna so the parents could watch *Bellbird*.

Of course, there was good music: Bowie, Blondie and Skyhooks among many others. Until 1977, there was Elvis. It was also the era of punk and disco – a miraculous time in which both The Sex Pistols and Donna Summer could flourish. And there was Australia's never-ending love affair with ABBA, who became the first group since the Beatles to replace one of their own songs ('Mamma Mia') with another ('SOS') in the number one spot on the Australian charts. In fact, by this time ABBA-mania had spread to almost every country in the world, so it was officially a pandemic.

During my adolescence in Canberra, people would go dancing to ABBA at the Roxy Bistrotheque – a unique combination of a bistro and a discotheque. Where else could you enjoy a chicken schnitzel, before working it off with a series of *Saturday Night Fever* moves? Maybe the CSIRO should release it as a diet. Or you might choose the Copacabana in Dickson, which featured a large, outstretched fibreglass hand in which the

DJ nestled, or perhaps the Chick Inn Video Disco in Jamison, or the Denim Disco at the RSL in Civic, or even the Private Bin, otherwise known as the Rubbish Bin on account of the unsavoury types who gathered there late at night.

As with television, memory tends to wipe out the musical dross that was on offer at the time. The biggest hits of 1973, for example, include Michael Jackson's 'Ben', a saccharine love song sung to a pet rat (which was eight weeks at number one); Tony Orlando's lachrymose narrative 'Tie a Yellow Ribbon' (seven weeks); and Col Joye's perky 'Heaven Is My Woman's Love' (two weeks). Meanwhile, in 1974, the two biggest hits were both by Paper Lace – 'Billy Don't be a Hero' and 'The Night Chicago Died', both eight weeks at number one, although honourable mentions should also go to Alvin Stardust for 'My Coo Ca Choo' (seven weeks) and Carl Douglas for 'Kung Fu Fighting' (three weeks).

Others eschewed buying singles, preferring to save up for a compilation record of the year's greatest hits – usually packaged with an excitement-filled title such as *20 Electrifying Hits*, *20 Dynamic Hits* or *30 Explosive Hits*. Among the classics of the genre: *Full Bore 1979*, which came with a free poster of a wild pig; and *Ripper 1975*, *Ripper 1976* and *Ripper 1977*, all of them with covers featuring a young woman in a pair of extensively torn hotpants, the hits written in pen on her bare arse-cheek. (No, really. Look it up.)

Whatever your musical taste, it could be satisfied via a number of different technologies. The least successful was the cassette tape – used to record favourite songs from the radio, or to pirate a whole album from a friend wealthy enough to buy one. Chief among the problems: the tape would stretch if left in the sun, an inevitability during a long road trip. You could start out on a summer holiday with something upbeat by the Bee Gees and drive home to a selection of Gregorian chants. The plastic box in which the cassette was packaged was cunningly designed so that all the pressure was placed at the weakest point – two tiny plastic hinges which would snap if you stared at them too long – plus a surface that accumulated scratches in a way that made the information impossible to read. After three weeks in the glovebox of the car, it was impossible to tell whether you were about to play Beethoven's Third or Blondie. With home-made tapes, there was also no space for a track listing, so people would do their best with a Biro using tiny letters. Bands with long names – Earth Wind and Fire, The Captain Matchbox Whoopee Band – would have their identity reduced to an incomprehensible series of initials. It's not by chance that the most successful band of the cassette age was ABBA: at least you could fit the name on the packaging.

Also, to use a cassette, you needed to keep a pencil handy. (Don't understand? Ask someone over 50.)

Others preferred LP records. The upside was that LP technology allowed a whole lot of pleasurable faffing around with accessories through which one could establish one's audio-bore credentials. There was the dust brush, the static cloth and even the 10-cent coin, which could be used to weigh down the needle to push through a particularly bad scratch. Even more importantly, record covers were large enough that you could leave them hanging around the house to impress visitors for whom you harboured romantic yearnings. Through the correct placement of the sleeve, you could show that you were cool (David Bowie), stylish (Roxy Music) or gay (Bette Midler). The need to turn the record over every 15 minutes also allowed you to stand, move away, discretely rearrange your clothing, then sit down again, but this time three centimetres closer to your intended love object.

On the negative side, records would develop deep scratches, which would result in the one musical phrase being played for eternity. With many of the musicians of the late 1970s, you were left wondering: is this record scratched or is he just being innovative?

*

Entertainment also came in the form of board games. The most popular local board game was Test Match Cricket, which featured tiny plastic players who, via a series of levers, could be made to bowl and bat in a way that was totally unconvincing. It was considered enormous fun, but only when compared to Squatter – 'the Australasian farming board game' – a version of Monopoly in which one would pretend to be a sheep farmer.

Among the items included in every game of Squatter:

- Six drought marker discs
- Five worm control program cards
- Five control-of-weeds/insects cards

Every 'chance' card represented a setback. With one spin of the dice, your bores would dry up; with another 'wild dogs kill many sheep'; with a third, you'd be injured in a tractor accident and be required to 'miss 2 throws'. The aim was to irrigate one's paddocks, much as you'd collect houses and hotels in Monopoly, but the real purpose was to finish the game while still believing that life has some meaning. Squatter was essentially propaganda for the farming sector; it made you want to immediately vote for the Country Party.

A number of other games were played during the period, and indeed are still played today. All had their drawbacks.

Game: Monopoly

Danger Area: Unattractive behaviour when victorious.

Monopoly was like alcohol: it brought out your innate

personality, which, for most people, was 'awful'. Many children, when facing defeat, would upend the board and storm out of the room. Even worse: when winning, it was almost impossible not to permit yourself the odd smirk. Or 'unattractive cackle' as one of my fellow players put it to me at the time. Through assiduous skill and the careful purchase of houses and hotels, a top player such as myself would be able to construct a series of attractive and adjacent holdings, thus forming a Zone of Death through which my opposition would be forced to travel, ground into the financial dust, round after humiliating round. (Cue unattractive cackle.)

Usual outcome: The loss of at least a couple of friends.

Game: Scrabble

Danger area: The three-toed South American sloth, the 'ai'. Did it really exist or had your charming competitor just made it up? Had she ever actually seen an 'ai'? And why was she so particular about it having three toes? Do most South American sloths have only two toes? If you had two three-toed sloths – or for that matter, three two-toed sloths – would you be able to just add an 's' and get away with the word 'ais'?

Usual outcome: Loss of prospective girlfriend.

Game: Five Hundred

Danger area: The counting of tricks by only one member of a couple, leading to the unwise phrase 'I just can't believe you didn't realise the 10 of hearts was still out there.'

Usual outcome: Loss of girlfriend or wife. Lifetime playing Solitaire.

Game: Trivial Pursuit (and its precursors)

Danger area: Smug, cocky walk to the fridge by Uncle Barry, just because he was the only person in the room to know the name of the currency of Swaziland.

Usual outcome: Uncle Barry no longer invited to Christmas. Dies alone. Only later does the family realise he'd amassed a large fortune, trading in international currencies such as the Swazi lilangeni, the profits all now bequeathed to the local dogs' home. Years of bitter recriminations.

Game: Charades

Danger area: Required to act out the cartoon title 'Fat Cat', the split-second decision to signal "first word" and then point at one's prospective girlfriend's bottom.

Probable outcome: 'Book', 'five words': *The End of the Affair.*

All in all, you'd be better off with an X-box.

One more thing. We had Scalextric cars. They always came off on the bend.

*

Others spent the '70s reading books. The books of the time were often quite peculiar. Conspiracy theories abounded, as did a sort of cheap mysticism. It was the period of Uri Geller, who would bend spoons, and Doris Stokes, who would commune with the dead on the *The Don Lane Show* – the perfect location for such an activity. As the British writer, Francis Wheen, put it: the '70s were 'a pungent melange of apocalyptic dread and conspiratorial fever'. I was myself addicted to the works of Lobsang Rampa, a Tibetan lama who related his paranormal experiences while growing up in a mountain monastery. The only problem: Lobsang turned out to be an English plumber by the name of Cyril Henry Hoskin, who had never been to Tibet and didn't speak the language. Lobsang wrote 19 books, mostly in the '60s and '70s, all bestsellers. One of them, *Living with the Lama*, was described as being dictated to Rampa by his pet Siamese cat, Mrs Fifi Greywhiskers. I was nothing if not gullible.

Lobsang put in a good effort but it was nothing compared to Erich von Däniken, whose *Chariots of the Gods* could be found on every '70s bookcase. A thief and fraudster, von Däniken worked up the theory that early humans had enjoyed contact with powerful alien civilisations. He found proof for the theory in the Egyptian pyramids and in Stonehenge – both of which, he argued, could only have been built with the assistance of futuristic technology. He also searched through ancient art, claiming that various squiggles represented space helmets, alien flying saucers, or Space Food Sticks. (Okay, I made up the last one, but the rest of it is straight von Däniken). The science writer Carl Sagan responded by calling von Däniken's success 'a sober commentary on the credulousness and despair of our times'.

I never fell for von Däniken but I did have a taste for some of the other bestsellers of the 1970s, none of which have been popular in the years since. Among them:

- John Fowles's *The Magus* (1965). Loved it when I read it in 1974. On a more recent reading: mendacious drivel.
- Robert M. Pirsig's *Zen and the Art of Motorcycle Maintenance* (1974). Loved it when I read it in 1975. On a more recent reading: incomprehensible twaddle.
- Erich Segal's *Love Story* (1970). You'll have to excuse me, I seem to have something stuck in my eye.

Strangely, despite the paucity of good things to read, we all wanted to read *fast*. Of all the '70s fads that came and went, speed reading was one of the most intense. Speed reading, much like polio, has now been eradicated in most of the First World, but, back then, everyone believed that reading *War and Peace* in two and a half hours was an excellent way to pick up its many nuances. In fact, bookshops in the 1970s consisted of little else other than books on mysticism and copies of Evelyn Wood's *Reading Dynamics*. No one thought to ask the obvious question: if speed reading works so well, how come no one has time to read anything other than books on speed reading?

All in all, is it any wonder that we'd rather focus on a really good backyard burn-off?

INTERMISSION

Fifteen Things Worth Reclaiming from the '70s

This book is largely a brutal attack on the past, challenging us to overcome our nostalgia and instead be optimistic about how the world has changed for the better and how it might continue to improve. All the same, some things about the period were just excellent. They need to be reclaimed.

The Pub with Nothing but Beer
Some years ago, there was a choice of 'New' or 'Old' and a built-in ashtray at your feet. Ask for a red wine and the barman would root around for the single bottle of shiraz, which he

would finally locate in the fridge. Service was brisk and there was never a queue. Now – all these years on – there's a wine list, divided as to region and a cocktail menu that runs to four pages, causing a scrum five-deep while five friends dither over whether to order the Negroni or the Caprioska, while the barman attempts to locate his 10th bucket of sliced lemon. This, ladies and gentlemen, may not represent progress.

The TV Program *Countdown*

We don't have a generation gap any more. That's because grown-ups claim they just really love 'young people's music'. That's because they haven't heard any 'young people's music'. *Countdown* would provide the necessary exposure to the awful reality. Bring it back.

Keeping Things for 'Best'

A set of cutlery for 'best', a set of plates for 'best', a set of wine glasses for 'best'. A whole front room for 'best'. All of it never, ever, used in 60 years of marriage. Still, it gave you something to put in the dresser and to hand on, in perfect condition, to the kids.

The Basic Appetiser

No wonder today's hosts look exhausted by the time the guests arrive. They've been in the kitchen since noon doing innovative things with West Australian crab. Only problem: your friends won't take any notice of all that effort as they down three glasses of chardonnay and try to remember each other's names. Reclaim the cabanossi and cheese on a cracker. Throw in a slice of pickled cucumber if you're up yourself.

Live Music in Pubs

Reclaim. Reclaim. Reclaim.

Restaurants that Don't Echo

Okay, in the 1970s, there weren't that many restaurants. But at least those that existed had carpet, tablecloths and curtains. You could hear yourself talk. Today we find ourselves in an echoing minimalist cube, stripped of all soft furnishings, no curtains, no carpet, no table-cloths, the music turned to loud. Admittedly, the hipster waiters have voluminous beards, but that's the only acoustic baffle on offer. Only by insisting the waiters circle the table – plaiting and braiding and caressing their luxuriant growths for the duration of the meal – do we stand a chance of being heard. Would it kill the restaurateurs to bring back a curtain or two?

Real Books

I understand the convenience of the eBook, but what about the role of the physical book in the art of seduction? Martin Amis understood this, back in the days when he wrote entertaining novels. In *The Rachel Papers*, a young man prepares his flat for the arrival of the prospective girlfriend, placing impressive books face up on the bedside table so as to convince her that he is a sensitive intellectual. Try that with an iPad. What are you meant to do? Invite the poor person to peruse your recent downloads? I attracted my own partner, Debra, by decorating my digs with the complete works of Joe Orton and Doris Lessing, and organising things so that, when she first entered the room, I'd be lying shirtless on the bed idly reading a biography of Chekhov. (I realise it's a disturbing image, but I was thinner then.)

Drive-in Cinemas with a Family of 12, Most of Them Hiding in the Boot

Such sneakiness, it's true, made it hard for the proprietor to turn a profit. Then again, the proprietor made most of his money from fining people who drove off with the speakers still attached. Bring back the whole glorious system.

Jeans that Look New when First Purchased

Pre-torn? Pre-faded? Pre-washed? No wonder, in the Bangladesh factories where this work is carried out, they think Westerners are a bit weird. Let's prove that Australians, inspired by the Anzac spirit, are still tough enough to wear out the knees on their own pair of jeans.

A Glass of Water when You Got Home from a Walk

The '70s was not only The Land Before Avocado, it was also The Land Before Hydration. People didn't hydrate, although they might occasionally slurp from a bubbler. This is in sharp contrast to today, when people will hardly leave the house unless equipped with the sort of water supplies normally associated with Rommel's African campaign. Water from a tap: bring it back.

The Effortless Holiday

When did holidays become so exhausting you needed 10 months back at work to recover? Back then, a holiday meant two weeks at Forster doing nothing at all. Now, it means a hike up the Andes to visit Machu Picchu, your experiences recorded in daily Instagram updates. Or you might prefer a European holiday which, for those who can afford it, involves going to countries so cold that you are forced to spend every available hour in a café or a restaurant, eating large quantities of overpriced food, while snow and ice hurl themselves at the windows. Who knows if such travel broadens the mind? It certainly broadens the buttocks. Bring back a week up the coast!

Supermarkets with no Choice

There's now too much choice when you are shopping. Do top loaders and front loaders really require a different formulation of sudsy stuff? Do we need dog biscuits offering specific concoctions according to the age, breed and personality type of the dog? And at what point did the purchase of milk become a way of expressing one's deeper life journey – 'Brad and I prefer the A2 protein, homogenised yet organic, in a light-to-medium formulation, from cows who've willingly agreed to the process of milking.' There are people on Tinder who've chosen a new partner in less time than it now takes me to buy a bar of soap.

'Just a Coffee, Thanks.'

Back in the 1970s, we understood that coffee was merely a beverage. We didn't obsess about it, banging on about *our* barista and how he achieves the perfect 'grind', and oh, oh, oh, don't even start me on his 'tamping'. Many are the times I have visited the coffee shop with orders from work: 'I want one latte and one flat white.' Normal people, by which I mean people not driven insane by coffee fetishism, understand that these two drinks are pretty much identical. It's like going up to a bar and ordering, with ponderous precision, 'Mate, I'd like one schooner of Tooheys New, plus I'd also like one schooner of Tooheys New.' The bartender would then pour the beers and, looking you firmly in the eye, point to the first beer and say, 'There's your Tooheys New, mate, and this one here' – he'd point again – 'That one's your Tooheys New'.

The Local Hardware Store

The place was tiny, but they always had what you wanted. Ask for a Furtwangler toggle, in imperial sizing, and the guy just reached into a drawer behind the counter. Usually, he didn't even have to move his feet. Now, the hardware store is the size of an aircraft hangar and yet, curiously, it never has the one thing you need.

Colour

Colour was everywhere. In the '60s and '70s, hardly any bathrooms were white. Instead the bath, hand basin and toilet were in matching colours, often with matching fittings. A light green was popular, and so was pastel pink and baby blue. The go was to buy your loo paper in the same colour as your fittings. One friend had what her parents called 'the galah bathroom' – pink all over, with a grey ceramic toilet-roll holder and a grey ceramic soap dish. Presumably, white bathrooms existed, but I can't remember any. Maybe people thought they'd show the dirt.

The only downside was the loo mat. For generations, men of all races have shown poor aim when approaching a toilet bowl, but it took the Anglo-Saxon world of the 1970s to come up with a response to the problem. Arise the fluffy, foot-warming rug, cut to fit around the base of the toilet, and ready to soak up any misfires. 'Why don't we create a moat of damp tufted polypropylene upon which you'll have to step in order to approach the facilities?' said some genius, yet to be identified. 'Good idea,' chorused the nation, installing the offending items in countless bathrooms, always in a colour to match the fittings, and usually teamed with a fluffy, elasticised seat cover that fitted over the lid. No wonder the women of Australia looked a little tight-lipped by the end of the decade. They'd spent a decade unable to get close to a loo.

More Colour

Kitchens were even brighter. White was available for kitchen appliances, but so was colour: harvest gold, turquoise green and coppertone. One of the main Australian manufacturers, Electrolux, introduced its 'New Generation' range in 1975. It was available in classic white as well as copper and poppy red. The latter is described in the company's advertising as: 'The shining warm colour that makes the kitchen snug and enjoyable and that spurs beauty in carpentry and textiles.' In the same year, Vulcan Chef was offering its new oven, the 'Parisienne', available in yellow ochre, burnt orange, red, avocado, lime green and coppertone. Whether Vulcan Chef's burnt orange oven would clash with Electrolux's poppy red rangehood, I cannot be sure.

Toasters were also coloured – red and sunburst yellow were common, but so was a white toaster with a bucolic scene involving chickens or pigs painted on the side. Actually, most things were available in what was offered as 'a range of colours'. For example, a 1975 digital clock was available in avocado, hot orange or white; the Ronson Carve 'n' Slice electric knife came in either beige or avocado; and tuxedo jackets suitable for a wedding could be obtained in a range that included maroon, bottle, navy and purple. Purple!

Terrible Schools

Schooling was essentially a blur of rote learning interrupted by the occasional brutal flogging. After 12 years of this torture, it was bliss to move on to even the most dismal of workplaces. No wonder everyone now is so dissatisfied with life; it is downhill from the second they come back from schoolies.

CHAPTER SEVEN

Buying Time

Flipping through old magazines, one thing keeps catching my eye: the advertisements mention price with a prominence that is rare today. 'The Ten Cent Extravagance', is the headline for a 1972 advertisement for flagon wine, which goes on to suggest that, at this rate, you might have a glass or two every night. 'Kayser Kapers are the wickedest underpants you can put on – and only cost $1 a pair.' There are also regular recipes featuring 'dollar dinners', calculated at 25 cents a serve for a family of four, Frankfurters and SPAM both making a regular appearance.

I'm not saying we were all dirt poor; nor am I saying that everyone now has it easy: the price of today's housing is a terrible daily burden, particularly on younger Australians. All the same, buying normal household goods in the '70s was a big challenge for nearly all families. Even a middle-class columnist like Ross Campbell would litter his pieces with references to the monthly payment on items such as the family fridge. In one column from 1970, he mentioned with pleasure the 'purple certificate' issued by one of the department stores when he managed to pay off his TV set. Credit was called 'buying on the never-never', and came in various arrangements. 'Lay-by' meant you reserved the item at the shop – perhaps a pair of slacks or a set of sheets – then paid a visit to the store each week, handing over a regular instalment, only taking possession of the item when you'd paid off the full amount, normally after six weeks. Or you could go for 'hire purchase', in which you were permitted to make use of the item at the same time as you paid off both the item and the usurious interest rate. It was also standard practice to rent household items such as fridges, washing machines or televisions. In the case of the TV, some families rented the set for a special occasion: once the Olympics, or the footy finals, were over, it would be returned.

Life was expensive. In his book, *Enlightenment Now*, the Harvard scholar Steven Pinker has this example: In 1919 an average American had to work 1,800 hours to pay for a refrigerator; by 2014 that average American had to work fewer than 24 hours to achieve the same purchase – which, by this point, was frost-free and had an icemaker. Certainly, in the Australia of the late '60s the purchase of a fridge was an achievement to be celebrated, particularly by recent migrants. Historian Alistair Thomson has observed how often photographs – designed to be posted to relatives back 'home' – featured a family member standing by the new fridge. 'They would open the door of the fridge when they took the photograph', he noted, 'so they're not just showing the fridge but also the plentiful food that was available in Australia.'

It wasn't only the fridge that required a savings program. Christmas required a concerted effort. Australian banks still run 'Christmas Clubs' – special accounts that penalise withdrawals before December – but they are no longer so ubiquitous. The ANZ Bank advertised its club under the slogan 'It lets you put Christmas on lay-by'.

The coming of colour television brought a similar offer: readers of the *Canberra Times* in 1974 were invited to set up a special 'Bank of NSW Colour Television Target Savings Account' so they might buy a set when the new system arrived on 1 March 1975. Few managed to save the necessary cash: by the end of March 1975, less than four per cent of households had upgraded to colour.

They just need to save a little harder. Luckily, the Home Hints column in the *Australian Women's Weekly* was there to help:

> A full-length winter night gown cut to shortie length leaves enough spare material to sew matching pillowslips at no extra cost.

That was $2 to Mrs M. V. Malan of Mackay, Queensland.

Another contributor noted that a nice sundress could be made by stitching together old tea-towels. Or from another:

varnishing children's school bags and hats could 'greatly extend their life'. ('Mum, my hat hurts.' 'Just pull it down hard, it will soften over time.')

Down in Tasmania the mania for saving money reached its high point in a local hero called Marjorie Bligh, whose money-saving hints appeared in all the local newspapers. Among her suggestions:

EYEBROW LINER MISSING? Don't worry. Take a match, the bigger the better. Burn the tip of it until black, then let it cool off. You can use it on your eyebrows like a pencil liner.

Or:

ROUGE: If you are out of rouge, cut a beetroot in half and use the cut side on your cheeks.

Or:

GREY HAIR CURED: Grey hair can be removed with a brewed-up mix of tea and dried sage, applied to your head every day until 'the right shade is reached'.

You can also, Marjorie advised, pour instant coffee over your head for similar results.

Marjorie's column became a clearing house for the ideas of Australia's tightwads. Consider this tip, supplied by 74-year-old Dorothy Redburn of Burnie, Tasmania, and sent to Marjorie for use in her column. Dorothy had a bra in which the elastic had gone, but the cups were fine. 'She cut away all the perished elastic at the back', noted Marjorie with admiration, 'and sewed in its place some heavy duty elastic bandage that she once used for a sprained muscle on the leg. She now just slips the brassiere over her head like you would your frock.'

Lovely! One day, after saving all those pennies, that colour telly will be yours.

*

On the upside, it was much harder to get into trouble with credit. Nearly everyone was paid in cash. The folding stuff arrived in a fortnightly delivery, served up at the pay window of wherever you worked. In my case, at the *Sydney Morning Herald* in the early '80s, the delivery point was a small square window, complete with metal grille, carved out of the wall of the seventh-floor corridor. You'd queue for a fair time – the only period the journalists and the printers spent time chatting together – and were then handed an envelope with the exact amount in cash, down to the last 45 cents. However poorly you were paid, the wad of twenties made you feel momentarily rich: 'It burnt a hole in your pocket', to quote an expression of the time. The aim was to get the money to the bank quickly enough so that it didn't combust entirely en route. At this point, Australia's banks only opened for three minutes a day, so timing was everything.

The notes themselves were cherished, so much so they were given affectionate nicknames. The $20 note was a 'lobster', and the $50 note – introduced on 9 October 1973 – was a 'pineapple'. Gulgong, near Mudgee, called itself 'the town on the $10 note' – a tourist campaign that imploded when the Reserve Bank changed the note's design. I guess they had to repaint the notice on the highway: 'The Town Once on the $10 Note'.

At the arse-end of every fortnight, there was an enforced period of fasting, sobriety and clean living. In the absence of credit cards, people would find themselves hunting for coins down the back of the couch or in the footwell of the car. If you are wondering why obesity is a post-'70s phenomenon, I have the answer. For the last three days of every fortnight, no one ate.

*

Jokes about smashed avocado aside, younger Australians – the so-called millennials – often claim their parents had it easy. Houses were cheap, employment involved full-time jobs, not the balancing act of part-time, gig-economy, rapidly evaporating jobs that make up many working lives today. There's much truth in this, of course. The rate of home ownership peaked at 73 per cent in 1966 and did so for a reason: with thrift and luck, most people could afford to buy a home. But the thrift was real. After the mortgage was paid, not a lot was left. At the end of the '70s, Hugh Mackay sat down with a sample of middle-class suburban families and asked them about their finances. 'In some ways it was a depressing study,' he wrote in his postscript. Much of the unhappiness came down to the impossibility of 'making ends meet'. Mackay tried to tease out people's attitude to saving but discovered the topic held little interest for his subjects: 'The question of whether money should be saved or spent is a question which simply never arises for many middle-class Australian families.' Money was spent in the week it arrived.

He then recorded some direct quotes from his participants, as they talked of the realities of family budgeting in 1979 and how often the burden fell on the women:

> My husband is a steak man, and that's that. He says he
> works hard and he has to have a steak every night. I
> think his manhood depends on it, or something. So the
> kids and I have to settle for the cheap cuts.

> When I think of us scrimping and saving and going
> without things for so long just to get into our own home,

and then not having a stick of furniture for the first twelve months. I think we were mad.

We were down to sausages a few weeks back, but even sausages are too dear now, and I'm having to look at some of the really cheap cuts.

If I didn't give my husband a decent meat meal once a day, there'd be hell to pay.

We've gone from forequarter to sausage-meat – I have to dress it up in a lot of different ways so that the kids won't complain.

People were nervous, and maybe not surprisingly so.

It's not that Frank's job is threatened, but with so many people out of work you never know what's round the corner.

The unemployment rate, as the 1970s came to an end, was 6.3 per cent. There was no routine superannuation. Inflation was high, at 9.1 per cent. Interest rates on a home loan were about the same. As Mackay noted in the postscript to his report, most people were gripped by financial anxiety. The only solution, for some of Mackay's participants, was to dream of a lucky break:

I'll tell you the sort of thing I mean – I know a bloke who just happened to see a Fiat for sale. It was parked in the street, the engine had seized, and he made the bloke an offer of $75. He fixed it up and sold it for $1200. But most of us don't have that kind of luck.

Despite the lack of money to spend, manufacturers kept coming up with novel products – hoping to tempt consumers into action. The '70s were the starting point for many inventions that would end up taking over the world. The first call on a mobile phone was made in New York City on 3 April 1973. One of the first personal computers, the MITS Altair, was promoted on the cover of *Popular Electronics* in January 1975. More to the point, the Breville Snack 'n' Sandwich electrical press was released in 1974 – and, within a year, was in one in ten Australian kitchens.

But the '70s also gave birth to a whole raft of products which left consumers underwhelmed. My adolescence was full of them. For example, quadraphonic sound. This was the 'future of sound' for all of five minutes. As with the later debacle over VHS and Beta, there were three different decoding systems and a paucity of quadraphonic records. Plus, given the music of time, did you really want four different speakers all playing 'Tie a Yellow Ribbon Round the Old Oak Tree'?

It was the same search for cutting-edge sophistication that led to the great bidet boom of 1974, in which French-style bum-washers were installed in Australia's more aspirational bathrooms. The next year they were all removed, along with Gough Whitlam and his ministers, after people realised they didn't know what they were for (the bidets, not the ministers).

The bidet, for some reason, was seen as sexy and thus connected with the free-love movement of the 1960s. The 'permissive society' reached Australia about a decade late, and even then in a diluted form – rather like a cyclone that had degenerated into a tropical depression. What began as wild sex and lefty politics in San Francisco manifested, a decade later, as a Saturday-night game of Twister played with Brian and Susan from around the corner, followed by a hangover and a bad case of cystitis.

To jog my memory as to the other product disasters of the time, I spent another morning back with my old friend, the leather-bound volumes of the *Australian Women's Weekly – 1970 January to December*. Every second advertisement, I discovered, was for a product that no longer exists. Whatever happened, for example, to freeze-dried instant tea? Back then, it was being sold with brassy full-page colour advertisements. 'Bushells Magic Spoonful,' said the headline in April 1971, 'the New Way to Make Tea.' Then the body copy: 'No waiting to brew. No tea leaves. The strength you like. The flavour you want. And so refreshing you feel better already.'

Or there was the K-Tel Record Selector, which 'works like a computer' but was really just a series of plastic slots into which you'd place your records. It offered little more than could have been achieved by leaning some LP records against a wall. The Singer Memomatic was similarly advertised in July 1972 as 'the new knitting computer', although with both products I have doubts about the level of computing power on offer. Mumble 'What's the square root of 99?' when standing in front of either device and see how you go.

Some products were even more obscure. The Sing-o-Ring radio was a luridly coloured transistor radio from National, worn on your wrist like a giant plastic bangle. It was halfway between a broadcasting device and a nasty growth. Then there was the Namco Sun-n-Slim Lounge – a banana lounge that converted into an exercise machine – in order to 'get rid of that spare tire and help improve your bustline'. Not bad for $49.95. Dacel Disposable Fancypants, meanwhile, were disposable underpants designed for daily use: 'Strong enough to stand up to all the things a girl gets up to in a day.'

Admittedly, just occasionally, there were moments of real breakthrough – like the moment in February 1970 when John West announced that fish would henceforth come in a ring-pull can, doing away with the old system involving a key. Suddenly, history was made.

Oh, to be sitting in a pair of Dacel Disposable Fancypants while tucking into an easily opened can of tuna. Life in the 1970s certainly had its attractions.

Dacel Disposable Fancypants are here. Jump into a new pair everyday.

Jump into Dacel Disposable Fancypants in the morning, jump out of them at night. Next morning jump into a fresh pair. You'll be treating yourself to a brand new pair of pants every day. Fresh clean feeling. And not extravagant.

You see, Fancypants are made from an amazingly strong new miracle fabric, known as "Dacel". Soft, comfortable and thoroughly reliable. They're economical enough to throw away. Strong enough to stand up to all the things a girl gets up to in a day. It's almost a shame to throw them away.

Available from chemists, variety and food stores.

You could get thrush just by looking at them.

*

Here's the downside: the Disposable Fancypants, I hate to tell you, were not made out of cotton. They were fashioned from an artificial fibre called Dacel. You could develop thrush just by looking at them. The advertisement, though, was very positive: 'You'll be treating yourself to a brand-new pair of pants every day. Fresh clean feeling. And not extravagant. You see, Fancypants are made from an amazingly strong new miracle fabric known as Dacel.'

Publications from the early 1970s are full of the names of synthetic fibres like 'Dacel' – some familiar, others that, like Dacel, appear to have disappeared into the clothes bin of history. There was Dacron and Rayon and Spandex; Bri-Nylon, polyester and Terylene. Also: Crimplene, a fabric with a sufficiently comic name that Barry Humphries made it Dame Edna Everage's fabric of choice. When people write about the history of Australian fashion, they usually mention the visit of Jean Shrimpton – a British model who wore a shortish white dress while watching a horse race in Melbourne in November 1965. Mostly forgotten is the fact that she was sponsored by the American chemical giant Du Pont, which paid £2,000 for her two-week visit. The shortness of the dress – a few inches above the knee – was the bait. The hard-sell was its chemical composition: it was made of Orlon – chemical name polyacrylonitrile – an acrylic fabric which Du Pont manufactured right up to 1990. As *The Washington Post* put it when Orlon was finally discontinued: 'We won't miss it. We wouldn't miss Ban-Lon or Dacron or Nylon either. They're made-up fabrics. One day they're a shirt, the next day they're a landfill. They look like something else. They feel like something else. They act like something else. And in no case are they as good as that something else.'

Despite all that, Australia's passion for synthetic fibres could not be stopped. We supplied the whole world with wool, and half the world with cotton, yet couldn't wait to dress ourselves in

Newspix

Jean Shrimpton thrills the nation in 1965. Just don't let her near a radiator.

what were effectively mulched up plastic bags. Why did people think these new materials were better than cotton and wool? The answer was: 'Drip Dry'. You didn't need to iron them. In fact, if you tried, they'd melt. Just walking past a radiator could cause people to burst into flames.

*

As a tightwad, I still have many of my clothes from the 1970s. Even trousers that no longer fit are still there in my wardrobe. Years ago, in the book *The Dag's Dictionary*, we had a word for this sort of clothing: it was 'Hope Couture'. It falls under the general rubric: 'Who knows? One day that diet might work.' In fact, schoolfriends meet me and often say, 'You haven't changed since school.' This is because I literally haven't changed. I'm still wearing the same shirt. Sure, my hair is grey, and my face is hideously wrinkled, but at least the outfit is the same.

I spent my teenage years wearing jeans and this particular flannelette shirt, before deciding to break free of my blandness through the purchase of a Mr John and Merivale Bri-Nylon one-piece zoot suit in white with tiny black pinstripes. The outfit consumed my first six pay packets as a part-time shop assistant and was appalling beyond imagining. It was the sort of outfit Elvis would have worn had he fallen on hard times and decided to take up work as a children's clown.

I then found full-time employment and had to buy a proper suit. I still have it – a garment, as usual, untroubled by natural fibres. They may have used cotton to sew on the buttons, I cannot be sure, but that would be the only concession to the world of nature. By noon each day, I smelt like a pig wrapped in plastic. After some reflection – reflection being easy to achieve in fabric that shiny – I decided to buy a second outfit. By this point, I was putting on weight – but only on my body. In my mind I was still thin.

I went into David Jones and picked a trendy English suit. The upside was that it was made of wool. The downside was that it was tailored for someone 10 years younger and 10 kilos lighter. The David Jones lady, God bless her, gently removed it from my hands and guided me to the Fletcher Jones section: 'We find these locally made jackets are better suited to our broad Australian shoulders.'

What a goddess that woman was.

*

The whole point of men's fashion was to remind a bloke how good looking he was, at least on those occasions when he glanced in a mirror. Meanwhile, the whole point of female fashion was to snare a man. 'Make the style suit the marvellous man,' ran the headline of one story in the *Australian Women's*

Weekly, on 4 February 1970. 'Is he romantic? Is he suave? Is he a swinger? Is he shy?' The magazine then presented a series of male types, suggesting the look that might appeal to each – from the managing director to the scientist. The scientist was particularly tough to attract: 'You'll have to be pretty striking to compete with nuclear fission.' The magazine recommended 'a geometrical hair-do with a black plastic dress'.

Or from an advertisement from the edition of 13 May 1970:

MAN-TRAPS: The gear that gets your man. Is he playing hard to get and you've tried every trick in the book? Try one more. Spring a man-trap on him.

This leads to some body copy in which the reader is urged to 'cage him in stripes' and 'knock him dead in Nylon', with the final sales pitch: 'Poor boy! He doesn't have a chance'.

Sounds good, but how easy was it to achieve this remarkable power over men? The mini-skirt, adopted nationwide after Jean Shrimpton's visit, was worn with cork-soled clogs and a fair bit of swagger. Australian women became the world's most enthusiastic supporters of the trend – wearing the skirts longer (in terms of the lifespan of the trend) and shorter (in terms of the amount of leg on display) than anywhere else in the world. Even as late as 1979, Hugh Mackay interviewed groups of mothers and daughters – discovering that while the daughters had embraced the longer skirts by then in fashion, they would nonetheless modify their school tunic to create an instant mini.

The mothers were not impressed:

> She's amazing – she wants all her hemlines down as long as possible at the moment, except for her school tunic which she seems to want up around her bottom.

Or, from another:

> They all want to have their school tunics up like the old mini-skirts – but they wouldn't be seen dead in other dresses like that.

Or another:

> She has her tunic up so high that, every time she turns sideways, you catch a glimpse of her panties.

Aside from the mini-skirt, the knitted pantsuit was popular, as was the colour yellow. Couples found delight in wearing the same pattern, including matching colours; and there was a trend for mothers and daughters to dress identically. An ultra-wide belt, called the 'wench-belt', was the perfect way to display a thin waist. Then, of course, there was the poncho – seen as the marker of

Crocheting was one way to fashion a man trap.

a person who reached out to other cultures and understood the variety and beauty of human experience. Unfortunately, in practice, it looked like you'd stuck your head through one of Mum's old blankets.

*

Fancypants to one side, consumer goods – from clothes to fridges – were always expensive and sometimes poorly made.

Throughout the '60s and '70s, many Australian industries were sheltering behind high tariff walls. In his documentary series *Making Australia Great,* George Megalogenis used the P76 – a car made here by British Leyland – as an example of all that was wrong with Australia's cossetted, tariff-protected economy: an economy in which companies were invited to operate without any effective competition.

Was the P76 that bad? The motoring writer Tony Davis put it this way: 'Every P76 seemed to have a unique combination of faults … rust, internal draughts blowing in from huge gaps in the panels and poor sealing, myriad squeaks and leaks, smouldering carpets (due to a poorly insulated exhaust system), interior fittings that shook loose and fast-deteriorating paint.' Owners, when presenting the car for warranty work, decided it was quicker to list the things that *didn't* need fixing, wrote Davis. The vehicle, in popular discourse, was rapidly renamed the Leyland P38 – 'Only half the car it was supposed to be' – and it soon went out of production, taking the rest of the company with it.

Despite such debacles, like many Australians I still believed in protectionism. In the late '80s – a decade and a half on from the P76 – the Hawke Government started to slice into the tariffs on clothing and footwear, tipping thousands of people out of work. I thought it was appalling: shouldn't everyone want to buy Australian-made? I had fierce arguments with friends, in which I'd say things like 'I don't care if I can only afford to buy three shirts, as long as they are Australian. Who needs 10 shirts, all of them shipped in from China?' I'd then defiantly stick out my chin.

I was rather missing the point. For a start, new jobs did eventually emerge for the textile workers, many of them involving higher skills and better pay. It was also easy for me to be sanguine about overpriced shirts. I didn't have kids; I was on a reasonable wage. It was different for people with children. In many families, there was rarely a pair of shoes that was not passed from one child to another. Younger children would often leave home as adults before ever wearing a new piece of clothing. And sheets – this was standard – would be used until holes appeared in the middle, at which point the sides would be sewn together to make a new middle.

There were joys aplenty in this era of make-do and hand-me-downs, but it also meant wearing underwear that had seen better days and swapping your socks so your big toes didn't align with the holes. No wonder a pair of Dacel Fancypants took on an aspirational aura.

Populist politicians – Donald Trump is the latest example – still flirt with the idea of tariff walls. I just wish he, and all the others, could first pay a visit to 1970s Australia. There, they'd find the reality of the protectionist world: it's an Aussie bloke bent over the engine of his stalled P76, constantly pulling up a pair of undies with too much give.

CHAPTER EIGHT

The Smorgasbord or
the Straitjacket

Australia in the '70s wasn't a great place to be a woman, a fact we dealt with in Chapter Two, but it also wasn't a great place to be a man. Or gay, or black, or a migrant. Actually, it wasn't a good place to be different in any way. We'll come to those other things shortly. Let's start with being a man.

At school in Canberra in the 1970s, being a man seemed to involve an attitude to women I found troubling, an attitude to sport I've never understood, and an attitude to alcohol which, well, I've been working on. Masculinity didn't seem like a smorgasbord of choices, it felt like a straitjacket. There was only one way to be male. And if being a man meant subscribing to this great long list of attributes – sporty, bit sexist, often drunk – what did it mean if I couldn't sign up? That I'm not a man?

I had a penis and at least a suggestion of chest hair, so what was I? Faced with this conundrum, I formed the view that I must be gay and tried my best to find other men attractive. At least being 'gay' was a thing. After a few noble attempts, I failed in my endeavour. So, what was I? An effete, book-loving, theatre-adoring, Bette Midler-listening heterosexual. Was that even possible? Could it even exist? In 1970s Canberra? Basic answer: yes ... but it felt unlikely.

Looking back, I should have been grateful I was not actually gay. For all my hopes, being gay was immensely difficult in the '70s. Homosexuality was illegal in every state, in line with public opinion. In 1972, a poll found that 65 per cent of people were against decriminalisation. In 1973, members of Sydney's nascent gay liberation movement picketed the Macquarie Street offices of Dr Harry Bailey, later infamous for his deadly work at Chelmsford Hospital. At this point, Bailey was using psychosurgery to 'cure' homosexuality – removing the 'homosexual part' of the brain. In at least one case, the man had been referred to Bailey by the courts. Bailey was happy to assist: the patient was 'a homosexual who desperately wanted help', Bailey told the *Canberra Times* in 1974, as he batted off criticism that his methods were leaving patients with reduced mental capacity.

Less tragic, but more common, were problems with employment. People were often sacked if they came out as gay: take schoolteacher Mike Clohesy, who was interviewed on television in 1975 as secretary of the gay lobby group CAMP – the Campaign Against Moral Persecution. Clohesy's comments were cautious and considered. Nonetheless, he was rapidly sacked by his employer at Marist Brothers Eastwood after 'parents complained bitterly about having a homosexual in the school'.

Clohesy gave evidence about his sacking to the Royal Commission into Human Relationships – a Whitlam initiative in which three commissioners took evidence on matters such as sexuality, women's rights and the status of migrants. The Royal Commission's final report, issued in 1977, summarised the employment situation: 'Governments, both Commonwealth and State, appear to be the most reluctant to employ homosexuals, particularly in education departments, the diplomatic service and above all, the armed services'.

The Royal Commission also listed the penalties in place for homosexual acts: from Western Australia where the penalty was 14 years hard labour, with or without whipping, to Victoria, which waived the whipping in favour of a sentence of 15 years. At the time, only one state – South Australia – had decriminalised the offence, the law changing on 17 September 1975.

The difference in legislation between South Australia and the rest led to some strange legal outcomes. In late 1975, a Victorian court considered the case of two men caught having sex at home. The court came up with what you might think was a novel punishment. The men were effectively deported to South Australia.

Yes, I know. Tough sentence. You'd rather the whipping.

Actually, the sentence may have been a blessing. Since they were sent to the only place in which they were allowed to live without persecution, it was a reward rather than a punishment. The ABC reported the case on its *PM* program in April 1975. I'm troubling you with the full transcript because it so thoroughly sums up the time.

Two Melbourne homosexuals have been given what amounts to an order to leave the state or face a gaol sentence. The two men, who had lived together for about six months, were arrested and subsequently pleaded guilty to charges of gross indecency and buggery, crimes for which the maximum penalty are three years and fifteen years respectively. The judge eventually released them on bonds of $100 with the proviso that they leave Melbourne for South Australia, where homosexual relations in private between consenting adults is not a crime. They were also directed not to live together until they left Melbourne.

Reporter (David DeVos): John, you say that you and Lindsay have been living together for nearly six months. How was it that you finally came to the attention of the police?

John: I was dobbed in by what I thought was a friend. It was only, I think, through jealousy on his part, about Lindsay.

Reporter: Was this third person the only person who knew about your relationship?

John: He was.

Reporter: Well, when did the police come?

John: He'd been visiting that night and he'd been gone about three quarters of an hour. Then there was a knock on the door ...

Reporter: The police came at night?

John: Yeah. And he flashed his badge and he asked if he could come in. And then he asked if I'd go into the bedroom of the flat with them, away from Lindsay.

Reporter: And why did he want you away from Lindsay?

John: Well, that I don't understand. I don't know because it was both of us involved. He called us in separately into the bedroom.

Reporter: Then what happened?

John: He said he'd come over because of a complaint he'd had, that we were homosexual. Of course, I made the mistake of saying yes and just answered his questions yes and no, truthfully.

Reporter: Did he ask you details of your personal life with Lindsay?

John: He did, after he asked us if we'd accompany him
down to the Vice Squad in North Fitzroy. And he
asked us those questions there. He didn't ask us
anything like that at the flat. They made it appear as if
it was nothing. I think that's what made me, you know,
just tell the truth.

Reporter: So, you told them everything, did you?

John: I did. All the intimate facts. Everything with it.

Reporter: Didn't you worry about legal representation at
that stage?

John: No. Well, I understood that if we weren't interfering
with anybody else we were alright. They'd come in
answer to a complaint and that person would have to
come forward and make the complaint against us in
the court. I didn't know the police would act against
our statements to get us into court.

Reporter: To your knowledge, has anything happened to
the third party who was involved in this?

John: Nothing. He's still running around bashing the beats
and everything the police are really against.

Reporter: Well, after this you went to court. You
appeared in court. Lindsay, what was that like?

Lindsay: Frightening.

Reporter: Why?

Lindsay: People looked at you and …

Reporter: Could you describe the attitude in the courtroom?

John: The barrister, after he had asked us the preliminaries, were we guilty or not guilty, we pleaded guilty. And the barrister stood up and started to say his bit and the judge just said, 'I've read the police report,' or whatever the police hand in, the briefs. And then he said, 'From what I can see these two are still living together so there's nothing I could do but send them to gaol.' All the judge kept saying was gaol, gaol. Lindsay was …

Reporter: He kept interrupting the barrister and saying, 'Gaol, gaol'?

John: Yes, he did. He wasn't prepared to listen. He did not want to listen.

Lindsay: And I just feel that, well, we were sentenced before we got there. Without a hearing.

Reporter: Did you go into the courtroom, with your barrister, with any defence in mind?

Lindsay: Yes, of course we did.

Reporter: What was it?

Lindsay: Well, that we weren't doing anybody any harm, other than ourselves. We were leading a life which we wanted to live. We weren't annoying anybody else. We had nothing to do with anybody else. We never went to any camp clubs or anything like that.

Reporter: Can you think of any reason that any of your neighbours might have had to complain about you and Lindsay?

John: None at all. We were striving very hard to get our own house, furniture, and everything else that we wanted and we were going along very well with it.

Reporter: Were you surprised when you were told, by the court, that you could either go to gaol or go to South Australia?

John: Well, really I was a bit disgusted. And I still … I don't feel guilty, I've got no guilt over it, but I feel a bit let down because of the way the judge acted.

Reporter: If the situation ever arose again would you tell the truth?

Lindsay: I wouldn't tell the truth ever to any policeman, whatsoever. I would tell lies, preferably to telling the truth, because you're far better off.

Reporter: How do you feel about each other?

Lindsay: I love John very much. In fact I love John more than I've ever loved anybody in my life and I think the world of him.

I can find no record of how the couple fared once they arrived in South Australia, but I do hope they found lasting happiness and I'm sure you do too.

*

Back in Victoria, the police were still hard at it. One 23-year-old, in 1975, escaped a prison sentence but only if he agreed to attend a psychiatry clinic. Another was fined, then turned up to work the next day to find himself unemployed; police had sent his employer all the court documents as an extra punishment. In the summer of 1976–1977, more than a hundred Victorian men were charged at a single location, Black Rock, after 'young policemen were sent to entrap homosexuals'. The quote is from a recent report by the Human Rights Law Centre, *Righting Historical Wrongs*, which includes details of the hundreds who were charged in the 1960s and 1970s. You certainly didn't have to do much to raise the ire of society. One student, Terry Stokes, a PhD candidate at the University of Melbourne, was fined $75 in 1979 for kissing his boyfriend in public. Soon after, Stokes was evicted from the college at which he lived. More than 100 men and women staged a 'campus kiss-in' in an attempt to force the university residence to reconsider its decision. That time around, no arrests were made.

It wasn't much better in New South Wales. In 1976 the New South Wales Vice Squad made at least 184 arrests. In 1978, at the first Mardi Gras parade, activists wore fancy dress and masks in order not to be recognised. Police attacked and 53 arrests were made, events dramatised in the 2018 ABC television program *Riot.* The *Sydney Morning Herald* made sure it published the names, addresses and occupations of all those arrested.

Over time, the other states joined South Australia's 1975 lead and legalised homosexuality. Tasmania was last. It waited until 1997.

*

Being gay was one thing; imagine being Indigenous. I didn't think much about Aboriginal Australia until I left school and scored my first job. It was with the Queensland Theatre Company. I was acting in a couple of theatre-in-education shows, touring schools in the bush. With two other actors and a tour manager, we'd hop in a car and drive west – out into the cattle country of Roma, Charleville and Aramac. We'd be hosted by the local representatives of the Queensland Arts Council – the grandees of the town, grateful that a little culture was being supplied to their children. Sometimes they'd provide a buffet – delicious! – then a drive around the district. All these years on, I can picture myself in the car, back seat on the left, while our host pointed out the local massacre sites: 'The Aborigines had staged a raid and killed a family of four. So, there was a retaliation and everyone in the Aboriginal camp was killed. It was just down there.'

It was very plainly spoken. The lady said 'Aboriginal' not 'Abo'. She didn't say, 'They were right to do it,' although that was implied. It was said as if it were just a part of the local geography – here's the pub, here's the river, here's the Aboriginal massacre site. That same scene, with slight variations, played out in several other towns. Later when I went to university, inspired by these matter-of-fact accounts, I wrote my history honours thesis about the racist science that underpinned such massacres. It was later published in a collection titled *Maps, Dreams, History: Race and Representation in Australia,* alongside a history thesis by Noel Pearson, who later became a significant Indigenous leader. When conservative commentators such as Keith Windschuttle started denying that many massacres had occurred, I thought, 'Mate, go to the bush and ask people, black and white. It's not that long ago. They all remember.'

Back in Queensland in 1977, race was everywhere. As a travelling crew of actors, we'd always stay in the local pub – $12 a night, including a cooked breakfast, sometimes prepared on a wood-fired stove. In most of the pubs – certainly the ones out west – there'd be a front bar for the white customers and a back bar for Aboriginal customers. I never saw trouble, I must say, but I also never saw much intermingling.

To be an Aboriginal Australian in the 1970s was to walk one of the world's roughest roads. All these years on, the road has remained rough. The gap in life expectancy between Indigenous and non-Indigenous is still a huge 10 years. The Indigenous employment rate is just 46 per cent, compared to

72 per cent for non-Indigenous Australians. Noel Pearson notes that Indigenous Australians are currently the most incarcerated people on Earth.

On the other hand, the number of Indigenous-owned businesses has grown 30 per cent since 2011, compared to a 1 per cent increase in non-Indigenous-owned businesses. The gap in life expectancy is coming down, albeit slowly. Pearson, when he talked in 2017 on the TV program *Q&A*, provided a list of problems – the incarceration rate, children alienated from parents, the number of youths in detention – before adding the caveat: 'We've made progress in the last fifty years'.

Life in Indigenous Australia is still tough, but it's difficult to contend it wasn't a whole lot worse in the past. For much of the 1960s, in much of the country, Indigenous Australians were not allowed to vote, drink alcohol, move around freely or cohabit with a white Australian. Aboriginal people were often barred from hotels and swimming pools in country towns, accommodated in separate wards in hospitals and in separate sections of the cinema. The law changed in various states and territories at various times. In the Northern Territory, for example, Aboriginal people were allowed to own property *and* sleep with white people – but only after the law was changed in 1964.

In 1965 the young Aboriginal activist Charlie Perkins initiated an Aboriginal Freedom Ride, targeting segregation and discrimination. His chartered bus, filled with students, visited many New South Wales country towns, including Moree, where Indigenous people were banned from using the local swimming pool. An attempt by the students to escort nine Aboriginal children into the pool resulted in the arrival of a crowd of 500 locals, who surrounded the students, shouting insults and throwing fruit. The fracas ended with the police forced to provide an escort for the bus so it could safely leave town.

Two years on, in 1967, the film *Journey into Darkness* was released. On the upside, it featured Indigenous characters. On the downside, those key roles were not offered to Indigenous actors. The Malaysian-born singer Kamahl played an Aboriginal criminal being hunted by an Aboriginal tracker. The tracker was played, in blackface, by Ed Devereaux, the dad in *Skippy*. Strange but true: attending the opening of *Journey into Darkness* was Harold Holt's last official duty before he ended his life by swimming out to sea from Victoria's Cheviot Beach on 17 December 1967. Coincidence? Or a desperate bid to escape?

Well, it beats the theory that he was picked up by a Chinese submarine.

*

In 1975 the Indigenous activist Bobbie Sykes gave evidence to the Royal Commission on Human Relationships:

Ms Sykes: I was born in Townsville and went to a Catholic primary school and convent there. I did well at school. I was in the top three right throughout the time I was at school, and I hoped to study medicine and be a surgeon.

Question: You were clearly unable to achieve this. Was there any particular factor which made it impossible?

Ms Sykes: They did not take blacks past fourteen in Queensland.

Question: So you found yourself out of school by fourteen, is that right?

Ms Sykes: That is correct.

Newspix

Having seen *Journey into Darkness*, Prime Minister Holt tried to make good his escape.

Later in her evidence, she listed the realities of 1975:

> We do not have a black doctor in this country. We do
> not have a judge or a magistrate or anything. We have
> what – a handful of black university graduates. Two
> hundred years? We just do not have an identity in the
> white society.

The first Indigenous doctor, by the way, was Dr Helen Milroy,
who graduated in 1983. The first Indigenous judge was Bob
Bellear, appointed in 1996.

*

Many decades on, I'm on Sydney radio with the Indigenous
leader Warren Mundine. I've always liked him, although he's
a controversial figure, too conservative for some. He's been
the federal president of the Labor Party, but also was recruited
by Tony Abbott as his advisor on Indigenous affairs. In this
particular radio moment, I'm quizzing the normally loquacious
advocate about his autobiography. I ask him about one scene,
involving his father. He gallops over it. Mundine is interested
in building bridges to the white community, rather than staying
too long in the past. Nonetheless, an autobiography demands
some attention to history.

'But,' I interrupt, as he rushes over his story, 'explain what the police said to your father that day.'

Mundine's story concerned his dad, a hard-working, conservative man who had – with enormous effort – managed to buy a house for himself and his family. They lived in the New South Wales town of Grafton and, in the early '60s, Mundine's father still needed a special pass to be out after 5pm.

One night, driving home with his son in the back seat, the police stopped the car. They knew Mundine senior. They knew he was a home owner. They knew he had what was called a 'dog tag', a Certificate of Exemption that allowed him, as an Aboriginal person, to move freely in the white world. It made no difference. They ordered Warren's father out of the vehicle then told him to take off his clothes. 'I peered around the back of the truck to watch him,' Mundine remembered. 'There was a look of wariness on his face – like he was wondering what was going on. But he remained silent and didn't argue with them.'

Warren, in his telling of the story, arrived at the point where he had to quote the words used by the police; the words he overheard as a little boy.

His throat seized up. Tears sprang forth. For a moment, he couldn't speak. Then, finally, he managed it.

'You might own a house,' the policeman said, 'but to us you're still an Abo.'

The year, according to Mundine, was 1961 or 1962.

*

There were other ways of being different. You could be a migrant. In the mid-1980s, as a young Fairfax journalist, I hopped a ride with a group of writers being taken by rail to the backblocks of Queensland. The group included Tim Winton, Thea Astley, Rodney Hall and a young Greek Australian poet called Komninos. The trip was full of memorable moments, but the highlight was a bloke who'd driven five hours to meet Komninos. 'I'm the only Greek within 400 kilometres of this place,' he told me. 'I just wanted to meet another one.'

Go back 20 years – to the mid-1960s – and that sense of isolation, of being one of a kind, would have been much more common – especially if you were not European. In the *Year Book* of 1965, the official statistical record produced by the Australian Bureau of Statistics, the text was enormously specific about the number of 'non-Europeans' living in Australia. According to the ABS, Australia was home to 76 Egyptians – 42 men and 34 women. They were so few in number, they could have been listed by name. There were also 101 'Asiatic Jews'. And 99 Afghans. Surely, I thought, the figures weren't really that low? Actually, they weren't. Just underneath, the ABS provided a second table. The first table, I came to realise, was just the 'full bloods'. The next table counted the 'mixed bloods' – half-European and half something else. With its assistance, you could add a further 27

Egyptians, 13 more 'Asiatic Jews' and 118 more Afghans – all in a nation just short of 11 million.

The 1965 *Year Book* also included figures from the 1954 census, at which point there were five women of African origin living in Australia. Really? Five? Who were they? Why were they here? What was life like for them? It seems like the starting point for a novel about isolation and despair.

A few years on, courtesy of the 1966 census, the figures were updated. There was a listing for those born in Australia – 81.6 per cent of the population – then a figure for 'Born in Britain'. These two numbers were then added together to give the figure for 'Total British: 11,039,387'. You could almost hear 'Land of Hope and Glory' playing in the background. They then threw in 'Foreign' people, mostly from Italy, Greece, Germany and the Netherlands. Another sum: 'Total Foreign: 511,075.' Those from Asia, the Americas, Africa and India – in fact from anywhere outside the 10 European countries considered worthy of separate listing – are recorded as 'Others'. They number fewer than 100,000.

Whatever the home country of the migrant – 'British', 'Foreign' or 'Other' – the welcome was pretty rough: an extended stay in some Nissan huts on the edge of town. It was difficult to get permanent work without a naturalisation certificate, and – as is still the case – difficult to have overseas qualifications recognised. Language differences were ignored.

In 1975, a consultant to the car maker Leyland gave evidence to the Royal Commission on Human Relationships about the treatment of the company's largely migrant workforce. All the workplace safety talks, he reported, were in English – 'the safety officer convinced he was getting his message across if he spoke in mildly accented English'. They then they 'took the migrants, put them in a booth and pumped English into the booth via a cassette loudspeaker. The induction speech, prepared by an advertising agency, mainly concerned the history of Australian cricket.'

No wonder the Leyland P76 had the odd problem.

Translation services, generally, didn't exist. In 1975 the country's biggest obstetrics unit, King George V hospital, had one part-time interpreter. He could apparently speak one language in addition to English, although – at this historical distance – it's unclear which one. In another hospital, a psychiatric facility, the head gardener doubled as the interpreter. The only problem – according to evidence given to the Royal Commission – 'he didn't work weekends'. Back at the Leyland factory, the consultant came across a Spanish woman in tears at her work station: it turned out she misunderstood what her doctor had said and had formed the belief her child had a fatal illness.

Many migrants decided they'd made a terrible mistake. My friend Rene, a Dutch Australian, tells me his mother cried for 'most of her first two years'. This may be an exaggeration, but you can imagine the sense of culture shock. The Australian Government had been actively recruiting migrants: they had a travelling display going to towns in Holland showing this affluent, cultured, generous nation. When the family arrived, including 10-month-old Rene, they were sent straight to the Scheyville migrant accommodation centre on the outskirts of Sydney. In Rene's words: 'Some rat-infested Nissan huts, each family area partitioned off with hessian sacking.' Rene, now a photographer, recently drove to the remnants of the camp, thinking he might capture the place in pictures, but found it all too sad and depressing. He and his parents lived there for three months. Rene's father eventually found work as a fitter and turner, his mother as a housekeeper, and they had the chance to move out and into the posh house in which Rene's mother now worked. 'It was my *Upstairs Downstairs* time,' he says.

Rene's wife, my friend Jurate, is from a Lithuanian background, but her experiences were similar. The family, including uncles and aunts, had qualifications, none of which were recognised once they'd arrived in Australia. Some ended up working as labourers creating Sydney's Warragamba Dam. They were young, she says, and did quite enjoy the use of explosives. Her aunt went to the Bonegilla migrant camp – notorious for its primitive accommodation and terrible food. Says Jurate: 'The main thing my aunt remembers was that the food was plentiful. In Europe, they'd been bombed. They'd been starving. She was grateful for the food.'

Jurate's family stayed, despite being slightly horrified by the paucity of cultural experiences on offer; Rene's family, after some decades, returned home. His mum, he says, still cooks the Australian-style meals that she'd learned – in a flurry of tears and anxiety – to keep her job as the live-in housekeeper. So, 65 years after her arrival in Australia, guests at An Vogelzang's home in Sneek, a town in the province of Friesland, in a country called Holland, are treated to meat pie, roast lamb with pumpkin, and – if they are damned lucky – a dessert of zesty passionfruit pavlova, the passionfruit smuggled in by her son on his trips 'home'.

Rene and Jurate live over the road from me in Sydney. My other neighbour, Domenico, has a different story. He came from Italy in 1969. Before then, he'd worked for eight years as an unpaid mechanic in rural Calabria. Since he was an 'apprentice', his various bosses decided he did not need to be paid. Tired of working for no money, he asked his aunt, already in Australia, to advance him his fare – $686 – and jumped on a plane. On arrival, he was given a one-day skills test by Australian officials. Presented with the engine of a Bedford truck, broken down into its component parts, he was required to rapidly assemble the motor. Then prove it would start. 'You are a good mechanic,' he was told after the engine roared into life. He was instantly presented with an Australian mechanic's certificate and was in work within a week. Within six months, he'd paid back his aunt for the air fare. Within five years, he'd saved enough to buy a house. It's the one over the road from me. He says now: 'I was very fortunate to come here.'

*

Some migrants, like Domenico, stayed the course. Others returned to their country of origin: that was the choice of around a quarter of the 'ten pound Poms', the assisted-passage migrants from Britain. Other families yo-yoed back and forth, changing their minds, pulled in two directions. There was, however, a third model. These were people who went home temporarily – but only in order to parade their success in the new world. This was my father's story. He and my mother had come out straight after the war – both from relatively poor families in the north of England. After stints in both Australia and Papua New Guinea, they'd done well. He'd become managing director of a moderately sized trade newspaper, serving the shipping industry. My father's sister remembers their visit, sometime in the early 1950s: 'They were appalling. Lording it all over us. I couldn't wait for them to leave.' All these years on, she still feels the sting of it.

Perhaps 'lording it over us' was possible in England, a country in which wartime rationing was still in place up to 1954. Europe was a different story: with the help of the Marshall Plan, it had rebuilt faster than anyone could have imagined. Those who fled to Australia felt they had left a smoking ruin, a place full of enmity, a battlefield that would never recover. Yet, by the time those post-war migrants went home to visit, much of Europe was looking pretty good. Those brave Australian migrants, who'd imagined they were sacrificing all for the sake of their children, returned to find that their nieces and nephews were actually pretty prosperous. Maybe more prosperous than their own children.

They shouldn't have believed those government posters.

*

It was worse, of course, for non-European migrants. Australia's most prominent news magazine, *The Bulletin*, had the slogan 'Australia for the White Man' blazoned across its cover right up until 1960, when it was removed by the incoming editor Donald Horne. The original version – Horne explained in his book *The Lucky Country* – was a response to Chinese immigration during the gold rush. It read: 'Australia for the White Man and China for the Chow.' If that seems hard to believe, it chimed with official policy. Until the mid-1960s, Australia's immigration law had an unabashed nickname: 'The White Australia Policy'.

I have an urge, at this point, to quote the famous phrase 'two Wongs don't make a White', expressed in parliament by Arthur Calwell, later Labor leader, but there's some complexity to the story: Calwell was debating a case involving an actual Mr Wong, and his opponent, from the Liberal side, was an actual Mr White. The newspapers, Calwell complained, didn't capitalise the 'w' in White. Calwell went to his grave saying he didn't mean it the way it sounded, but it is, and will always be, his most famous phrase.

Whatever the details, Australia operated an immigration policy explicitly based on ethnicity and did so with the agreement of both political parties. There was even a European dictation test, in which you had to prove you spoke at least one European language. It was a policy, incidentally and hilariously, used by the government in 1934 to block the entry of the European communist and multi-linguist Egon Kisch. The fine print of the dictation test didn't identify which European language was to be used, so officials tested the lefty troublemaker in Scottish Gaelic. He spoke 10 languages, but not that one. Ha, ha. Alas, for the government of the day, the Australian courts came down on Kisch's side – concluding that officials had made inappropriate use of the dictation test – and so he was permitted, on 17 February 1935, to address a crowd of 18,000 in the Sydney Domain. He used the speech to predict that Adolf Hitler was planning to start World War II. Yep, what a dangerous radical.

Despite such tussles, by the early 1960s the White Australia Policy was losing majority support, but only just. When, in a series of Morgan polls between 1960 and 1963, people were asked whether they agreed with letting in 'a reasonable number' of 'skilled' Asians, roughly a third rejected the idea. In 1971, when the research organisation ANOP asked whether people approved of 'coloured' migrants settling in Australia, there was a similar result – 35 per cent disapproved. Pandering to this view, the Australian Labor Party didn't remove its support for the White Australia Policy until 1965. Its vestiges remained until 1973.

*

Back in 1965, when people wanted discord, there was no one to fight with other than members of another Christian denomination. Still, Australians of the time made the most of it. Diversity meant a punch-up between the Catholic kids and the Protestant kids at the local train station. Roman Catholics were nicknamed 'Mick' (because many were Irish and had surnames starting with 'Mc') or alternatively 'Rock Chopper' (because the initials matched, besides which it was assumed they were all Irish navvies, employed to build roads by breaking up rocks). Protestants were called Proddies or Proddy Dogs or, if they were Presbyterian, 'Press-Buttons', which seems rather affectionate.

Frank Moorhouse, covering the 1972 election for *The Bulletin*, met the Liberal member for the seat of Macarthur, Jeff Bate. Moorhouse summarised the conversation: 'He was raised to hate Catholics, Victorians and rabbits and now he says he only hates rabbits.' Bate's wife, Dame Zara, widow of Harold Holt, was quoted later in the article: 'He doesn't really hate rabbits. He gets upset about poisoning them.'

Despite the ecumenical embrace practised in the Bate household – Catholics! Rabbits! All good! – relations between the Christian faiths were often problematic. Mixed marriages often created tensions, with relatives refusing to attend the service. Some Catholics believed you required the permission of your bishop before attending any form of Protestant service, including funerals and weddings.

Protestants were keen to return this sectarian hostility. In Melbourne, to quote writer Gerard Henderson, there was 'the Protestant ascendancy'. Business was dominated by the WASPs – White Anglo Saxon Protestants. In Victoria, they gathered in the Melbourne Club, located at 36 Collins Street, from which they ran nearly all the significant firms. Catholics, effectively denied entry to either the club or the world it controlled, would instead choose the professions – mostly medicine or law – or the public service. The latter had the advantage of an entrance exam in which your name wasn't included on the paper. Says Henderson: 'They couldn't tell if you happened to be called Patrick O'Sullivan'.

In Sydney, power was more equally shared. Even the department stores had religious convictions: Mark Foys was for Catholics; Farmers and David Jones were for Protestants. When the journalist Max Walsh was given a cadetship at John Fairfax and Sons – publisher of the *Sydney Morning Herald* – he was the first Catholic to be employed in that role in more than a hundred years. At the time, he recalled, it was impossible for a Catholic to be employed at David Jones. In 1974, Walsh was appointed editor of the *Australian Financial Review*, at which point he was the first Catholic to edit a major daily for Fairfax. Meanwhile, in the New South Wales Police Force, Catholics and Protestants (or, more precisely, Protestant Freemasons) took turns in occupying the position of Commissioner. It's a tradition that began in 1952 with the first Catholic commissioner and has continued, with only the occasional double-up, ever since.

Meanwhile, up in Brisbane, one Catholic remembers singing the chant: 'Proddy dogs, they jump like frogs'. In the spirit of balance, he remembers that there was a regular rejoinder: 'Catholic dogs sit on logs, and stink like frogs'.

*

All these years on, the tribal disputes between Catholic Australians and Protestant Australians appear fanciful – yet ask anyone of the right age, and they'll confirm it all happened.

Of course, as migrants began to arrive, the urge to demonise shifted target – first to Greeks and Italians (called Wogs and Dagos), later to people from Asia, then to those from the Middle East, and more recently to refugees from Somalia.

Of course, racism still exists in Australia. As an Anglo Australian, it can be hard to fully imagine the impact of its day-after-day grind. It's been particularly tough, recently, being Muslim in Australia. It's been particularly tough, always, being Indigenous in Australia.

On the other hand, it's important not to overplay the reach of this prejudice. Pauline Hanson's anti-immigrant, anti-Aboriginal rhetoric has never proved more than a temporary electoral success. According to a 2016 international survey by the Pew Research Centre in Washington, Australians are now among the most enthusiastic people in the world about migration – both refugee and skilled. That enthusiasm is reflected in the numbers who have been welcomed. The Bureau of Statistics calculates that 33 per cent of Australia's population was born overseas – ahead of Canada's 22 per cent, Germany's 15 per cent and Britain's 13 per cent. In Sydney, the proportion born overseas rises to 43 per cent. Almost 40 per cent of Sydneysiders speak a language other than English at home. In Melbourne, it's 35 per cent.

Those 'other' languages, by the way, are no longer all European. Of the 33 per cent of the population born overseas, the biggest group now comes from Asia. Non-Christian religions continue to grow: back in 1965, the *Year Book Australia* had no separate listing for any non-Christian group other than Hebrew: the numbers were so low, they were not worth counting. These days, Australia's 'Top Ten' religions include Islam (2.6 per cent of the population); Buddhism (2.4 per cent) and Hinduism (1.9 per cent).

Both in practice and when asked by pollsters, nearly all Australians have embraced the country's multicultural society. As I write this, there's a story in the news that, in a way, gives both sides: a 25-year-old man was arrested after a racially motivated rampage, targeting people of Asian background. The attack was horrible – slurs, spitting and punching. Yet the police arrested the offender after a group of appalled construction workers rushed in, tackled the man and held him down until the authorities arrived.

Australia, of course, still has arguments about migration, most notably over the harsh treatment of what the government calls 'illegal boat arrivals' – people who are dumped in offshore gulags to await an uncertain fate. Yet the popular support for the so-called Pacific Solution shouldn't blind us to the great enthusiasm of nearly all Australians for officially sanctioned forms of migration. Despite the occasional outbreak of tension – Sydney's Cronulla riots of 2005 are the worst example – few people in Australia's most ethnically diverse city would list 'racial tension' among life's problems. 'Traffic jams', 'pathetic public transport' and 'how do you get a good view at Mardi Gras' are all much higher on the list.

Then or now? Again, I'd rather now.

CHAPTER NINE

The Enlargers and the Straighteners

Some see the late '60s and early '70s as an inspiring, exciting time. There's plenty going for that idea. By that era, Australian films were being made in numbers not seen since the 1920s. A book industry sprang from nowhere. Theatres were suddenly staging plays written by Australians. In Sydney, there were Green Bans, led by the construction unions, which prevented the demolition of some of our most beautiful buildings.

It was a glorious period of firsts. The first lesbian rights lobby group, the Daughters of Bilitis, was formed in Melbourne in 1969. The first Aboriginal Tent Embassy was erected on the grass outside Federal Parliament in 1972. The first refuge for women escaping domestic violence, Sydney's Elsie, opened in 1974. Three internationally significant books were published within just five years, all written by Australians: *The Female Eunuch* by Germaine Greer (1970); *Homosexual: Oppression and Liberation* by Dennis Altman (1971) and *Animal Liberation* by Peter Singer (1975). And, of course, in 1972 the Whitlam Government was elected, ending 23 years of conservative rule, and introducing what felt like a million reforms. The end of conscription! Free university study! No-fault divorce!

What a time of glory.

There's another way of looking at all of this. The moments of change were startling because they occurred in a country that had resisted change for so long. To make a defiant stand, you need to face an opposing army. To win an historic first means fighting a battle no one has previously managed to win. Yes, it was inspiring that Jack Mundey's Green Bans saved the historic 18th-century buildings in The Rocks, yet how incomprehensible that – in the mid-1970s – the birthplace of Australia's European history was on the verge of being demolished to make way for office towers. And while it's wonderful to recall the first flowering of Australian theatre at Melbourne's Pram Factory and Sydney's Nimrod, how depressing that – with a few notable exceptions – Australian stories had, for decades, been largely silenced.

In his book *The Lucky Country*, first published in 1964, Donald Horne fulminated against a country that 'has not got a mind'. A 'pall of ennui spreads over the suburbs', he wrote, a place where 'much energy is wasted pretending to be stupid'. He talked of 'a kind of Tariff Board approach' to art and literature, in which

Australian practitioners didn't even attempt to be as good as those from overseas. Two years later, when journalist Craig McGregor wrote his *Profile of Australia*, intellectual life remained thin on the ground. University students, McGregor wrote, came in for criticism from their elders simply for being students: 'They would be better getting on with some useful work instead of wasting their time with arty nonsense,' was, he said, the common view. Outside the universities, wrote McGregor, Australian intellectuals faced 'overt hostility'. Their operating policy was borrowed from James Joyce: 'silence, exile and cunning'.

For the most part, it seemed we had two kinds of culture: agriculture and horticulture. The culture of the mind was harder to locate. Despite the heroic efforts of firms like Angus & Robertson, most authors were driven overseas to find a publisher. Thomas Keneally, who later won the Booker Prize for *Schindler's Ark*, had his first novel published in Britain. Same with Patrick White. Same with George Johnston. True, there were local literary magazines such as *Meanjin* and *Southerly*, but authors preferred to sell their stories overseas. As Frank Moorhouse joked, 'Meanjin' was an Aboriginal word meaning 'rejected by *The New Yorker*'.

In lieu of any form of government assistance for the arts, the advertising industry provided succour to the country's would-be writers. Among them: Bryce Courtenay ('I'm Louie the Fly – straight from rubbish tip to you'); Peter Carey ('You make us smile, Dr Lindeman') and Philip Adams ('Guess whose mum's got a Whirlpool'). The ambitious headed overseas – Morris West to Rome, Clive James to London and Robert Hughes to a trifecta of Italy, London and New York. In truth, it would be quicker to list the significant Australian writers who stayed. Among those fleeing, at some point in the 20th century: Christina Stead, Lily Brett, Peter Carey, Germaine Greer, Clive James, Peter Porter, David Malouf ... well, you get the idea.

It was the time of the 'cultural cringe', to borrow the phrase minted by the critic A. A. Phillips – the tendency, still not extinguished today, for Australians to believe their culture inferior to that created elsewhere. In the *Australian Women's Weekly* in the 1970s, a two-page spread appeared every week under the headline: 'What They Are Wearing Overseas', in which a dozen women, mostly British, would be pictured wearing various outfits that aspirational Aussies might ape.

This love-in with the British affected more than the fashion pages. When Brisbane-born Richard Casey became governor-general in 1965, he was only the third Australian in the role. Previously, they'd nearly all been British aristocrats – including four barons, three viscounts, three earls and one duke. As late as 1967, Australian passports still bore the word 'British' on the cover. The value of the Australian dollar was shackled to that of the British pound: whatever the economic indicators in Australia, the value of our currency rose and fell to suit conditions in Britain. Weirder, in the run-up to decimalisation, the government seriously planned to call the new unit of currency a 'royal'. That proposal was abandoned after months of ridicule, thank God, otherwise you and I would be saying to this day: 'Mate, I need to buy a glass of chardonnay, could I borrow eight and a half royals?'

We weren't only craven towards Britain. Our politicians also had a slavish devotion to America. In June 1966, Australia's new prime minister, Harold Holt, visited Lyndon Baines Johnson in the White House and coined the phrase: 'All the way with LBJ'. Holt then proceeded to fulfil the promise he'd made, sending successive waves of young Australians to fight alongside the US in Vietnam. In the end, almost 60,000 Australians, including ground troops, air force and navy personnel, served in Vietnam. As a result of the war, 521 died and more than 3,000 were wounded.

Forget dollars, the initial plan was for a unit of currency called 'The Royal'.

Only later did historians realise the 'All the way with LBJ' rhyme would have worked just as well with a previous president: 'All the way with JFK'. Australia could have become a humble, fawning satellite some five years earlier. A few decades on, John Howard could also have tried harder. He committed Australia to the war in Iraq while neglecting the obvious rhyme: 'We love your tush, President Bush'.

*

Even when the school syllabus focused momentarily on Australia, the emphasis was on Australian failure. In my schooldays, all our heroes were losers. For inclusion in the syllabus, the person had to have died a miserable death, preferably alone in the desert.

In the early '70s, we'd do a death a week.

Open your books, boys, today it's Ludwig Leichhardt.
—So, Sir, how did he die?
Miserable and alone in Queensland, boys. In this way he is quite
different from Burke and Wills who also died miserable and alone –
but closer to the centre. And to Sturt, who didn't die miserable and
alone, but did fail to find the inland sea.
—Thank you, sir.

Once a year, we'd study Gallipoli, usually around the time of Anzac Day. Gallipoli fulfilled all the requirements for inclusion: it was an inglorious defeat, in which the Australians showed courage and ingenuity while being needlessly slaughtered. Adding to the piquancy of the tale, it was all the fault of the Poms.

Later, we'd move on to other local heroes. There was Phar Lap, triumphant until poisoned by the Yanks; Captain Cook, triumphant until he was hacked to pieces by the Hawaiians; Ned Kelly, triumphant until he was hanged from the neck until dead; and Les Darcy, triumphant until he died from septicaemia due to some dodgy American dental work. Add in: Breaker Morant, court-martialled then shot by the Poms; Henry Lawson, drank himself to death; and John Curtin, died in office.

It wasn't just the schools. In Sydney, they named the airport after someone who died in a plane crash – Kingsford Smith – and the main road out of the place – the Hume – after someone who'd endured a lifetime feud with his co-explorer, William Hovell. (While the road is named after Hume, the adjacent public housing, of course, pays tribute to his colleague.)

In other parts of Australia, the list of failed heroes was slightly different. In Western Australia, schoolchildren would learn about the achievements of C.Y. O'Connor, the engineer who first piped water to the goldfields, allowing the state's economy to boom in a way that still brings riches today. Such success might have ruled him out as an Australian hero but – just in time – O'Connor, unfairly attacked by the Perth newspapers, rode his horse into the sea south of Fremantle and shot himself in the head. Naturally, the people of Perth eventually commissioned a statue of the man and had it erected on the spot in which he died. A miserable and solitary death? Mate, we find we appreciate you after all.

*

Theatre, in this period, consisted of touring companies from the UK doing British plays, or the J.C. Williamson company mounting Australian versions of foreign shows – a thriller from London such as *Sleuth*; a Ray Cooney farce like *Move Over Mrs Markham*; an American musical such as *Promises, Promises*. The shows featured mostly local actors, putting on British or American accents but, sometimes, the whole cast was imported. *The Black & White Minstrel Show*, for example, toured regularly from 1964 to 1970 – 'direct from London' – with full British cast, presumably because Australia's white actors couldn't pretend to be black Americans with as much authenticity as white actors from Britain.

The music scene was also dominated by foreign performers. Many big names toured during the period – The Beatles, Roy Orbison, The Rolling Stones, The Kinks – but Australia was also the place where fading celebrities could top up their retirement fund by slogging their way through a final tour. Jack Benny was 70 years old when he visited Australia, Gracie Fields was in her late 60s, and Nelson Eddy, a few years from death. So constant were such tours of the old and infirm that Barry Humphries saw the opportunity for a joke. When, in March 1978, Charlie Chaplin's body went missing from its grave in Switzerland, Humphries offered reassurance to the world: 'Don't worry. He's just touring Australia.'

Sometimes, the locals took offence at the attitude of the visitors. One of the best columnists of the period, Ross Campbell, was devastated when Noël Coward was quoted on his departure from Sydney airport: 'I like Australia and I love those wonderful oysters.' As Campbell complained:

> When we go to other countries, we take an interest in
> the people. We don't say: 'I like Scotland. It has such
> wonderful cows.' Or 'We loved the USA. The bears are
> fascinating.' We are only human. We like ourselves to be
> noticed, as well as our oysters.

His final point: 'No people have played second fiddle to their own fauna as much as Australians.'

This failure to appreciate the Australian people was especially apparent among the visiting 'stars' shipped out for the annual Logie television awards. In 1967, the choice was the American actor Vic Morrow, who stood there, mute, handing out the prizes. The local compere, Burt Newton, later recalled the embarrassment: 'Every so often, I'd say, "How are you going, Vic?" and he would just nod his head.'

In 1973, it was the turn of another American actor, Michael Cole, who appeared to be drunk, managing to slip the word 'shit' into a mostly incoherent acceptance speech, the first time the word had been said on Australian television. Other visiting stars seemed uncertain as to their location – Australia, Austria, more likely Canada. 'Anyhow, love those Mounties,' was the gist of many a speech.

Sometimes, it must be admitted, we gave the visiting stars a poor experience in return. Marlene Dietrich visited in 1975 at the age of 74 and, in the opening moments of her Sydney show, fell from the stage into the open orchestra pit. She broke her leg so badly she never regained her ability to walk without a stick. Increasingly dependent on painkillers, she withdrew to her apartment in Paris and died, isolated and bedridden. The legendary British comic Tony Hancock made a quicker exit. His career was on the skids after he thoughtlessly sacked the two writers who'd made him funny, Ray Galton and Alan Simpson. He took his own life on 25 June 1968, in a basement flat in Sydney's Bellevue Hill, while filming a never-to-be-released Channel 7 series called *Hancock Down Under.*

Meanwhile, at local airports, fresh celebrities would arrive to replace the fallen. There, they'd be quizzed by a specialist airport reporter, who would greet the inbound foreigners and ask them, 'What do you think of Australia?' – this before they'd seen anything but the arrivals hall. The celebrities were required to say: 'Fabulous!' with as much sincerity as they could muster. The reporters would then press on with their follow-up questions, which became infamous for their pure daftness. Among them: 'How many members in your quartet, Mr Brubeck?'; 'How do you spell your name, Mr Sinatra?'; and, to a visiting Catholic cardinal: 'Is your wife accompanying you on this visit?'

*

The election of the Whitlam Government in December 1972 was Australia's attempt to break with this pathetic, stagnating period. Cultural cringe would be replaced with cultural pride. Australia would shift from inward-looking to outward-looking. The fawning over all things American and British would stop. There'd be a new attitude to Asia. It was as if we'd taken a look at a map and suddenly noticed our location.

The pace of post-election change was electrifying. While the final votes were still being tallied, Whitlam set up a cabinet of two with his deputy, Lance Barnard, and began implementing Labor's election promises. Their first decision was to abolish conscription. Next: steps necessary for the future introduction of colour television. Third, that women should have equal pay. The innovations continued as the new government settled in. In no particular order: free university education, land rights for Indigenous Australians, colour-blind immigration, generous funding for the arts, no-fault divorce and a 25 per cent tariff cut, the first move in the dismantling of protectionism.

Having sat on its hands for 23 years, the country was making up for lost time.

The only problem was that Australia, like the rest of the world, was then hit by stagflation. Inflation and unemployment were growing in tandem in a way that seemed to defy the economic models of the time. Worse, in October 1973, the Organisation of the Petroleum Exporting Countries (OPEC) increased the price of crude oil by 70 per cent. The effect was to create stagflation on steroids. It wasn't only us. Governments around the world entered a death spiral. Whitlam, perhaps aware of the looming problems, held an early election in 1974, in attempt to refresh his mandate. He won, albeit on a tighter margin, and returned to office convinced he had permission to keep spending. It wasn't the best decision. The economy started to look seriously unwell. The vultures began to circle, including the opposition leader, Malcolm Fraser, who looked a bit like one.

The opposition had already talked about using its control of the Senate to deny funding to the government – a threat so outside conventional Australian politics that Menzies, living in retirement, privately mused about 'the idiots that now run the Liberal Party'. Labor, meanwhile, was toying with an even stranger idea: borrowing a couple of billion dollars from Middle-Eastern countries – outside the usual systems – using the skills of a friend of a friend of a friend called Tirath Khemlani.

It was at this point that Fraser, employing his party's power in the Senate, refused passage of the appropriation bills – effectively starving the government of money. The governor-general, John Kerr, a man appointed by Whitlam, reacted by removing the government and appointing Fraser as caretaker prime minister. The date was 11 November 1975.

At 4.50pm that day, the GG's private secretary, David Smith, stood on the steps of the old Parliament House and in a high, nervous voice read the proclamation of the government's removal. Whitlam towered and glowered behind him.

The private secretary's speech ended: 'God Save the Queen.'

Whitlam took over and repeated the closing phrase: 'God Save the Queen – because nothing will save the governor-general.'

*

On 11 November 1975, I was a schoolboy living two suburbs away from Parliament House. As soon as I heard the news, I rushed down.

Being an adolescent in Canberra had many drawbacks, among them:

- The cold.
- The boredom.
- The lack of coffee at night (see Chapter Three).

But it did have this: parliament was close.

I missed the famous moment – 'Nothing will save the governor-general' – but, by the time I arrived, the crowds were growing in size and in anger. No one could quite believe it. We felt we'd witnessed a coup d'état. Donald Horne, writing soon afterwards, put it this way: 'The sacking of Whitlam had the shock of an assassination.' We all assumed there would be protests, a repeat of the marches that had helped end Australia's involvement in Vietnam. Maybe a national strike. Maybe violence. It was exciting and terrifying and baffling all at once. The crowd stayed late into the night, at which point the affable Fred Daly, legendary Labor MP, walked out onto the steps, gave a long, passionate, occasionally funny speech, and told us all to go home.

Then ... nothing happened. The people failed to rise up. There were arguments in every pub, and in front of every TV set, but that was as far as it got. No protests of any substance. No strikes. Stranger still, a large group of Australians, previous supporters of Whitlam, switched sides in the election of December 1975. According to Donald Horne, the thinking went this way: for the Queen's representative to sack him, Whitlam really must have done something wrong. As Horne put it in his book *Death of the Lucky Country*: 'There were enough authority-respecting Australians for them to change sides when a Governor-General had spoken.'

*

Decades later, on the 30th anniversary of the Dismissal, I had the chance to interview Gough Whitlam on my radio show. He was 89 years old, sharp and witty, filling the studio with his charm and charisma. Thinking it might be one of his last interviews, I asked about his school years. Was he sporty? 'I did rowing. It's good political training because you can look one way while going the other.' So, still hilarious.

Then, of course, I asked about Kerr. Gough described both Kerr and his social-climbing wife, calling her Fancy Nancy. He explained how Kerr, at one point, manufactured a trip to the UK just so Fancy Nancy could meet the Queen. Then Gough moved on to 11 November. As he recounted the events, I prodded him to repeat the famous words, said on the steps, after he took over the microphone.

'So you said?' I prompted …

Me and Gough, on the thirtieth anniversary of the Dismissal – but will he repeat the famous line I missed first time around?

Whitlam laughed. He knew exactly what I wanted – a repeat of those famous words – but first he wanted to set the scene.

'You'll remember,' he said, 'there was a squeaky voice' – this was a reference to the GG's secretary – 'followed by my voice which, at that time, was very good. The proclamation ended with the words "God Save the Queen" and I said, "Well, may we save the Queen because nothing will save the governor-general."'

He paused, savouring the recollection, then repeated: '... nothing will save the governor-general ... and it didn't! Because you'll remember he went into exile with Fancy Nancy' – a delicious, long pause – 'and what could be worse.'

Thirty years on, what sweet revenge.

*

The final chapter of the Whitlam experiment came with the post-Dismissal election, held on 13 December 1975. For all the outrage at the events of 11 November 1975, Whitlam was cast aside in a landslide.

Australian history, according to Manning Clark, is a perpetual battle between the Enlargers and the Straighteners. If this were so, the Straighteners were back in charge. It was too late, though, to stop the avalanche of change that Whitlam had begun.

Over the next couple of decades, Australia was to be transformed.

*

For the last year or two, as I've written this book, I've spent a lot of time in the early 1970s. The books and magazines of the time have been my constant companions. I've studied the politics, re-listened to interviews like the one with Gough. I've hectored my friends for memories.

Right now, though, my quest is coming to an end. It feels a little sad. I hate it back there, yet still don't want to say farewell.

Shouldn't I create some sort of last hurrah? Something that would be both an experiment and a celebration? Something that would help answer the central question of my quest: 'Was the past really that great?' Something that would bring a few laughs, alongside a few truths? I decided to hold a '70s dinner party. What would my guests, all these years on, think about the food? And what about the gender politics of the event? I invited two couples my own age, as well as two 20-something colleagues from work, Olivia and Serge. I composed a menu of delights. For the entrée: Smoked Oysters, Devilled Eggs, Cheese Log, Devils on Horseback and a pineapple bristling with toothpicks loaded with cubed cheese, cabanossi and brightly coloured pickled onions.

If that didn't stop them in their tracks, the main courses surely would:

- Emerald Surprise, sourced from the 1971 *Miss Australia Cookbook* – a melange of bacon, sour cream and thawed frozen peas, served as a salad.
- Apricot Chicken, made by my friend David, one of the evening's guests, and based on his mother's handwritten recipe – right down to the four tablespoons of cornflour.
- Spicy Meat Ring, discovered, as previously mentioned, in the free *Arnott's Crinkle Cut Potato Chip Recipe Book* of 1970.
- Mushroom Vol-Au-Vents, with store-bought pastry cases.

- And Potatoes Romanov – from the *Vegetarian Epicure*, a recipe book which, as noted earlier, appeared to have been produced as a way of assisting the dairy industry to get rid of excess product.

Then, for dessert:

- Pineapple Upside Down Cake, in which tinned pineapple slices are combined with unfeasibly large quantities of brown sugar.
- Marshmallow Viennese, in which sherry-soaked Marshmallows are combined with tinned crushed pineapple and unfeasibly large quantities of cream.
- After Dinner Mints, store-bought, of course.

Preparation for the party was enormous fun. Friends offered retro tablecloths, water jugs and salt-and-pepper shakers. There was also debate about how far we should go in the name of authenticity. Should I demand everyone take up smoking for the night? In 1970, close to half the crowd would have been puffing away. Should we hand-wash the dishes at the end of the night, remembering that mechanical dishwashers were rare? And should the men and women start the evening in two separate groups – the women busy in the kitchen, discussing salad and

Lord knows what else, while the men stood out the back, talking about the big issues of the day:

- Pacific Highway or New England? Which is the best way between Sydney and Brisbane?
- Ford or Holden? So how much mileage do you get out of a tank of petrol?
- That Junee Morosi? What do you reckon is going on between her and Jim Cairns?

Maybe not. We decided to limit the retro feel to the food and the tablecloth.

I went to the supermarket and bought up big, arriving at the checkout with the world's most embarrassing trolley load. So many canned goods! Such huge packets of chips for the Spicy Meat Ring! Two jumbo bags of marshmallows for the Marshmallow Viennese! I nearly explained my plans to a woman behind me in the queue, since she was eyeing off my haul with some curiosity, but I reconsidered. She'd only demand an invitation.

Debra and I cooked all day, dutifully following each recipe in turn, and occasionally pausing to say, 'Oh, surely not.' It was the phrase that greeted the whole cup of sour cream in the Emerald Surprise; the large quantities of ricotta cheese *and* cheddar cheese *and* sour cream in the Potatoes Romanov;

and the whole packet of barbecue-flavoured chips in the Spicy
Meat Ring.

The guests arrived, giddy with excitement. I offered drinks:
Passion Pop, a startlingly sweet carbonated wine first made in
the late '70s, and Mateus Rose, my father's favourite. Oh, and
Resch's Pilsner.

My 20-something producer Olivia gamely had a Passion
Pop. 'Delicious,' she said. I had a taste myself. I decided not
to trouble the bottle any further: a man my age could develop
diabetes just from the label. Other guests selected the Mateus.
'Only quite good,' was the general view. All the same, the night
buzzed with possibility. Some dishes, I was pretty sure, would
be a failure – the Spicy Meat Ring – but others would surprise
on the upside.

We moved to the table. I'd provided name tags so everyone
knew where to sit. The women were designated in an authentic
1970s way. There was Debra – 'Mrs Richard Glover' – at one
end of the table. Then my friends, Kerrie and Susanne, but here
transformed into Mrs David Chenu and Mrs Paul Andrews.
Their husbands were also there, but you should be able to guess
their names. Then the young people: Olivia was 'Miss Olivia
Shead' and Serge was 'Mr Serge Negus'.

After the entrée, I asked the guests to rank the dishes. Olivia,
a vegetarian, quite liked the Cheese Log, but was worried about
how I'd managed to press that much cheese into the shape of a

log. 'I kept imagining how it was made, and it freaked me out. I wanted to know whether you had washed your hands.' Exactly. Dealing with millennials. It's tough.

Serge, not a vegetarian, would surely come to my rescue.

'What did you think?' I asked.

He responded: 'The Smoked Oysters on Jatz crackers were good. I like a Jat. But I would give a zero to everything else. Even the Devils on Horseback. I'd rather the bacon on its own.'

I asked him about the Cheese Log.

'I was hoping it would be better than it was.'

Were the people my own age more positive? Not exactly. They liked the Devils on Horseback (a prune, stuffed with an almond, then wrapped in bacon) but almost nothing else.

Main course would surely be better. We started with the Apricot Chicken. It was terrible. All you could taste was cornflour. Next the Spicy Meat Ring, of which Olivia said, 'I've never been so pleased to be a vegetarian.'

Even the Potatoes Romanov, a dish I used to cook throughout the '80s, was indigestible. So much sour cream! So much cheese! A thought presented itself: 'Mystery surrounds the 1918 death of the Russian royal family, but this dish may explain it ...'

I conducted a final scoring. The Cheese Log came in last, with a points tally of two out of ten. The winner, startlingly, was the Spicy Meat Ring, which scored a somewhat respectable six.

'How did you enjoy the night?' I asked the two young people as they were leaving. 'Brilliant,' said Serge, 'I've never been to a dinner party where you were allowed to be so enormously rude about the food.'

Olivia concurred.

At least we had fun. I gave them all two Alka-Seltzer tablets on the way out.

CHAPTER TEN

The Rose-coloured Now

Nostalgia is natural. Writing this book, I kept feeling its pull. I would think about a song, some clothing, some food and it was hard not to sigh and think, 'Life was better then.' For a start, I was younger. I was thinner. Plus, some parts of life *were* better. The anxiety that has come with social media did not exist; nor did cybercrime. We were spared the house prices that crowd young people out of the market; we hadn't yet seen the casualisation of work. Most employees were in a trade union, which – most of the time but not all of the time – proved a good thing. There were fears aplenty – particularly of nuclear annihilation – but nothing to match what appears to be the current, avoidable own-goal of global warming.

For all those reasons, and a fair few more, there's a widespread resistance to the idea that things have improved – even though it's so spectacularly clear that life is much better now than it was. Does that matter? Should we care if people convince themselves that life is getting worse, both in their own country and in the wider world, even if that view is difficult to justify? Does it matter if people look at the past through rose-coloured glasses? I think it does.

This is only partly a book about Australia in the '60s and '70; it's really an argument about the possibility of progress; about how quickly we can change; and how things that now seem laughable or downright objectionable were considered normal just a moment ago. Most of all, it's an invitation to dream of further change. So, in case I've not quite won you over, here's a few more ways in which the past was not so great – and how committed Australians, with the support of the rest of us, changed things for the better.

1. The place ponged

When Whitlam came to power, many ordinary households were not connected to the sewer, especially in the newer, outer suburbs. In Sydney, around 100,000 septic tanks were installed between 1958 and 1970 – more than 11,000 in 1964 alone. In Perth, for instance, 72 per cent of houses were unconnected at the end of 1972. Those who didn't have a septic were instead visited by the 'night soil man', who'd remove the full pan, clip a lid on top, heave it on his shoulder, then jog it up the drive to his cart – in the process giving Clive James inspiration for one of the best scenes in *Unreliable Memoirs*. The pong of 'night soil' was part of everyday life. Even in a suburb connected to the sewer, you couldn't quite avoid the sewage. In Sydney, for instance, the partly treated effluent was pumped out near various beaches. One outfall was just 500 metres from Bondi Beach, a situation that led to the quaint warning for swimmers to watch out for 'Bondi cigars'. In Victoria, they called them Werribee trout or King River prawns. In Tasmania, a Blind trout. The names were quaint and creative, but all of them referred to the poo in which you were swimming.

Certainly, Whitlam himself regarded the provision of sewerage to ordinary working families as one of his most enduring achievements. As always, he's worth quoting: 'I found half the nation unsewered; I left it fully flushed.'

2. It wasn't just the sewer that lacked connection

In the late 1960s and early 1970s, many households lacked a home phone. Routine matters such as the summoning of a train driver to an extra shift, or a firefighter in an emergency, were done by telegram – an army of 'telegram boys' cycling around the suburbs. It wasn't enough to want a phone; you had to join the queue. Some tried to bribe their way to a connection – £100 was the going rate – but, if you were caught, you'd be back on the bottom of the list.

A waiting time of six months was common; in some suburbs, it was two years. Worse still, sometimes the answer was a simple no. Your application was denied with no possibility of appeal. These were called 'application deferrals'. In 1951, there were 128,000 people given the knockback; by 1971, the annual figure had reduced to 13,000 – still a fair number, considering these were people not even allowed to join the queue. After talking about this on the radio, a listener, Kevin Freund, sent in some correspondence from the time. His father worked for the railways doing emergency track maintenance and had made many rejected applications. In 1963, he tried again, this time with a supporting letter from his boss, who emphasised the importance of the emergency work done by Kevin's dad. The Postmaster-General still turned down the request. I have the letter: 'It is regretted the Department is not in a position to provide the desired facility at present.'

They weren't being mean. The exchange couldn't handle any extra lines.

Even for those lucky enough to have a phone, the experience had its limitations. In the country, people often had party lines – several households sharing the same service. The ring differed according to the intended recipient, but neighbours were also able to pick up and (quietly) listen to what was being said. Again,

I owe this observation to talkback radio: people with party lines became adept at listening for interlopers. Said one caller: 'Our neighbour always tried to listen in, but would be given away by her ticking kitchen clock. Another had an asthma problem.'

The result: 'George, I can hear you. I think you should hang up.'

Party lines were not the only limitation. Calls overseas had to be booked ahead of time, with the operator interrupting the call to ask if you wanted another – expensive – three minutes. Before the term 'STD' was associated with sex, it meant Subscriber Telephone Dialling, an amazing advance in which you could just ring interstate without requiring the assistance of the operator. It was advertised as a 'pay-as-you-say plan' and was available in all the capital cities by 1967. Despite the absence of the operator, it was still fairly expensive. In fact, up until 2009, any STD call was preceded by three beeps – just to warn people they were participating in a pretty boutique service and that they should take pleasure in their elevated station in life.

3. Kids were armed

When Debra Oswald, my partner, was 17 years old, she was shot in the bum with an air rifle. It was 1976. She'd been washing her dad's car, wearing her bikini and listening to Donna Summer on her transistor radio, when a stray pellet ricocheted off the neighbour's driveway and struck her hard. The neighbour's son had been practising in his front yard with his new weapon and had missed his target. Almost every element in this picture seems to be from a forgotten world. The transistor radio. Target practice on the front lawn. Certainly, the 17-year-old girl happy to wash her father's car.

Debra was fine, the stray pellet successfully removed from her bottom by the doctors at Parramatta Hospital. The neighbour's son, I assume, was told to restrict his activities to the backyard, nothing more. Guns, after all, were common. Even an effete boy like me was given an air rifle for my 11th birthday. Actually, for some reason, I had two. My neighbourhood friend and I would shoot cans in his front yard. Others shot birds. Now, some decades on, air rifles are considered Class A firearms, subject to Australia's strict gun laws.

The air rifle wasn't the only hazard on offer. Backyard pools were not fenced – in most states, fencing only became mandatory in the late '80s and early '90s – so suburban drownings were common. Cracker night, in which kids were encouraged to run around throwing bungers at each other, was a much-anticipated date on the calendar. Childproof lids weren't mandated, so poisonings were also regular events.

In Australia, official data about death is published in the wonderfully named *GRIM* books – The General Record of Incidence of Mortality. Accidental drownings, according to the relevant *GRIM* book, declined by 67 per cent from 1979 to 2015. Let's just consider toddlers – these days more than a hundred fewer drown each year, compared to 1974, despite the rise in population. For the same period, accidental poisoning, as a cause of toddler death, fell to one-eighth the previous level. The possibility of dying between the ages of 5 and 14 has nearly halved for Australians since 1990 – from 1.9 per thousand children to 0.9 in 2016 (earlier figures are hard to come by). The chance of survival for those under five years has been transformed since 1965. At that point, out of every 1000 Australian children, 22.4 died before they reached their fifth birthday, either from illness or accident. Now, the figure is 3.7.

My point: the GRIM figures are in no-way grim reading. It's hard to find a GRIM chart that doesn't show huge progress.

It's a trope of talkback radio that it was so much better in earlier decades, when children were allowed to roam and to take risks – 'We just had to come back before it was dark.' Playgrounds, people say, were also properly exciting – in this glorious time, before the fun police took over and removed the death-defying slippery dips, the merry-grounds able to fling a child into outer-space, and the giant rocket ships from which you could see your whole town.

Yes, lots of it was fun. Two points: children still manage to have fun. Many fewer die.

4. Crime was rampant

In the 1970s, we all knew someone whose car had just been pinched or whose house had just been ransacked. Such was the level of crime that householders became masters of deception. They'd never leave the house without leaving a radio blaring. There was a 'Beware of the Dog' notice on every front fence, whether they had a dog or not. There were size-11 workmen's boots left purposefully by the front door, as if just kicked off by a giant now reposing inside, his large legs akimbo.

When going on holidays, things became even more intense. Some householders took the family rubbish with them – worried the waiting bin would tip off thieves. Packing the car was another source of anxiety, as any activity might tip off passing robbers. Why did so many families leave at 4am? It wasn't only to beat the traffic. It was also because Dad – keen to defeat the thieves – wanted the whole operation to be conducted under cover of darkness. Silence and speed were the keys. Whispered voices would cut through the stillness of the night air: 'Gary, just get in the back with your sister and take this bag of prawn heads with you.' Others remember being required to carry their surfboards around the corner, standing in front of some random house, so it wasn't so obvious the family was leaving on a trip. Dad would then whip around the corner, put the boards on the roof rack, throw the kids in the back, and gun the engine for the Gold Coast.

I remain uncertain about the morality of this, since any passing thieves would presumably target the house in front of which the surfboard-carrying children had been instructed to stand. But these were strange times …

*

Ask people about the crime rate anywhere, anytime, and they'll tend to say it's going up. In recent years, that view has nearly always been wrong. According to Our World in Data, the compelling and authoritative website created by the German economist Max Roser, crime rose rapidly in many Western societies from the early 1960s onwards, before starting to fall just as rapidly in the early 1990s. By most measures, the rate is now lower than before it began to rise.

One of the most reliable indicators is the murder rate: in Australia it hit a peak of 2.16 deaths per 100,000 in 1973–74 and continued at a slightly lower level through the rest of the '70s and all of the '80s. In 1989–90, for instance, it was 1.8 deaths per 100,000. By 2016, it had dropped to an historic low of 0.9 per 100,000 – reflecting 227 deaths nationally. That figure would double if the 1990 murder rate still pertained. So that's 227 lives saved each year.

Or take armed robbery. In 1975 in New South Wales, there were 376 armed robberies – the majority using a firearm. Armed robbers attacked 19 banks, 28 chemists, 34 petrol stations and 32 taxi drivers. Street stick-ups occurred 71 times. The victims totalled 376 – 4 of whom were killed and 19 of whom were 'cut, gashed or stabbed'. Others were 'bruised'. What's changed? Experts cite better security, particularly for banks and cars; the shift from heroin to ice and cocaine (with the latter two drugs, you can sometimes still work); and consumer goods so cheap that it's hardly worth stealing them. Throw in the ubiquity of surveillance cameras, the effectiveness of DNA testing in catching criminals and the widespread use of credit cards rather than cash. The national gun buyback scheme in 1996 was also important – 600,000 firearms were removed from the community – but it wasn't the only factor. The level of violent crime has also fallen in nations that have made no change to their gun laws.

Murder aside, it can be hard to find reliable crime statistics from the '60s and '70s as they were often skewed by police departments, keen to look like they were winning 'the war on crime'. In New South Wales, that changed in 1989 when the incoming director of the Bureau of Crime Statistics and Research, Dr Don Weatherburn, won direct access to the police figures. Although he can't assist with the earlier period, he can be precise about the way crime in NSW has fallen from 1990 to 2017:

- Robbery with a firearm: down 90 per cent.
- Motor vehicle theft: down 82 per cent.
- Break and enter non-dwelling: down 78 per cent.
- Murder: down 69 per cent.
- Robbery without a weapon: down 64 per cent.
- Break and enter dwelling: down 64 per cent.

He has more, but you get the picture. It's frustrating to Don Weatherburn that such major changes are so little reported. The reason? People would always rather believe that things are getting worse, even when they are getting so dramatically better.

5. Corruption was common

I know what you are thinking: corruption is as bad as it has ever been. In New South Wales, Eddie Obeid, former minister and one-time Labor power broker, is serving a lengthy prison sentence. So is his colleague Ian Macdonald – known to colleagues as Sir Lunchalot. In the Northern Territory, the former police commissioner is serving time for attempting to pervert the course of justice. In Western Australia, it's a former council official in jail – sentenced to just short of two years for taking kickbacks. Surely, it's worse now than it was in the past?

Very unlikely. The Sydney of 1965 to 1975 was the Sydney of Robert Askin. He was premier for this whole period, and the town was awash with illegal gambling – with SP bookmakers and illegal casinos; with standover merchants and the cockatoos keeping watch at the corner. The whole corrupt edifice had a pinnacle – the office of the premier. On his death in 1981, *The National Times* calculated that Askin and his police commissioner, Fred Hanson, were both paid $100,000 in bribes each year from 1968 until Askin's retirement. The newspaper publisher Max Newton once described delivering, in 1970, a brown paper bag to the premier's office, a gift from a developer. He recalled: 'I've never seen $15,000 disappear so quickly in my life.' When Askin's widow died in 1984, she left an estate worth $3,724,879.

Things were just as lucrative in Queensland – the place dubbed the 'Moonlight State' by ABC TV's Chris Masters, whose investigations proved that corruption went right up to the commissioner of police, Terry Lewis. He'd been taking money since 1980. Jack Herbert, the bagman at the centre of the network, collected more than $3 million in protection money from gambling and prostitution, of which about $600,000 went to Lewis. The system was known to its participants as 'the Joke'. In return for immunity from prosecution, Herbert revealed the whole system to the Fitzgerald Inquiry into Possible Illegal Activities and Associated Police Misconduct. People still argue about how much of the money was shared with the politicians of the time. The premier, Joh Bjelke-Petersen, king of the gerrymander, saw two ministers and his police commissioner jailed, but his own trial for perjury was abandoned after the jury couldn't agree on a verdict. He was then judged too old to face a second trial. Bjelke-Petersen's 'minister for everything', Russ Hinze, also had health problems. He died before he could face charges for receiving corrupt payments of $520,000.

Of all the dodgy politicians of the period, there was only one I had the chance to meet. It was Rex 'Buckets' Jackson. In the early 1980s, as the New South Wales minister for prisons, he granted early release to selected prisoners upon payment of a small bribe. After being caught and convicted, he served five years in Berrima Jail, enjoying the hospitality of what had once been his own establishment. Later, he ran (unsuccessfully) for office and I spent a couple of days with him on the campaign trail. We got on quite well. Bad boy me, when he opened his briefcase to show off his campaign material, I peered in. I can still remember my surprise: several large rolls of $20 bills, each secured by a fat rubber band, just looking for a home. I imagine, after all those years behind bars, he was still waiting for a chance to spend his ill-gotten gains.

6. Bullying was considered normal

In workplaces and schools, sexual harassment was rife, as was the hazing of apprentices or newcomers. Sometimes, it was on the humorous side – the young guy on the team sent to the hardware shop to ask for a can of striped paint, ha-ha, or a left-handed screwdriver, ha-ha-ha. At the other end of the scale, it involved violence, often sexualised violence. Boot polish on testicles, heads being pushed into toilets, that sort of thing. There are no real statistics on this, partly because it was regarded as so normal. Ask anyone who was around at the time and they'll tell you some quite appalling story.

7. Death. Everywhere death.

Earlier on, I mentioned the increase in longevity, but the figures are so good I'll repeat them. In 1965 Australia, life expectancy at birth was 67.7 for men and 74.2 for women. Averaged across the genders, it was 70.85 years. Now, averaged across both genders, it's 82.5. That's nearly 12 years' extra life! Much of the improvement is down to better diets, less smoking, a bit more exercise and the advance of medical science. Some of it, however, is down to how dangerous and unregulated life was in the '60s and '70s. People now mock occupational health and safety rules which, admittedly, can be quite annoying. I've done outside broadcasts for the ABC, in which my chance of dying was closely examined by several layers of executives, even though it was just me and a very pleasant person showing me how to make cheese or knit a jumper. Really, what was going to go wrong?

Workplace accidents still happen today – each one an unacceptable tragedy – but in the past, workplace accidents were not only more commonplace, they were often bigger in scale. The West Gate Bridge tragedy in Melbourne – 15 October 1970 – took 35 lives. A mine gas explosion in Ipswich in 1972 took another 17. Another mine explosion in 1975 took 13. The Tasman Bridge disaster of 1975 took 12 more lives.

Sometimes, it was workers; at other times, customers. One rail accident – Violet Town in Victoria – took nine lives in 1969. That was dwarfed by the Granville train disaster in 1977: 83 lives were lost after the train hit a bridge, which then collapsed onto the carriages.

Building fires were much more common than today and far deadlier, largely because of the lack of fire safety equipment. Thirty homeless men died in a fire at the Salvation Army's William Booth House in Melbourne in August 1966. Another 15 died in March 1973 at Brisbane's Whisky Au Go Go nightclub; another 15 in 1975 at Sydney's Savoy Hotel. There are still urban fires, of course, but there are also fire drills and extinguishers, fire escapes and sprinklers.

For all the talk of 'It's occupational health and safety gone mad', we have a greater chance of surviving today.

8. Litter. Everywhere litter.

Australia still has a litter problem, but it's much better than it was. The verges of major highways were once a glinting necklace of smashed bottles and empty cans. You'd stop the car at some random spot and look out at a sea of boxes, milkshake containers and crushed cigarette packets. It was common – on highways and suburban streets – for people to stop their car, slide out the overflowing car ashtray, open the driver's door and tap the contents into the gutter. The whole country was spotted with these sad little piles of discarded butts.

Has it really got better? There are no figures from the '70s, which perhaps proves the point: who would have thought to commission such a study in a period when littering was so commonplace? More recently, a national litter index has been published by Keep Australia Beautiful. It shows a downwards trend – consistent for the last decade – which news organisations, as usual, have somehow managed to ignore.

9. You couldn't do anything on a Sunday

To do anything much on a Sunday was a desecration of the Sabbath. Prior to July 1965, Victorians were not allowed to screen movies. At that point, the law was liberalised: you could show a film, but only 'after Evensong'. The session times wouldn't be in that day's newspaper, because there was no newspaper. Sunday newspapers had been banned in Victoria under the *Sunday Newspaper Act* of 1889; a law that held sway until March 1969. As the writer Keith Dunstan noted, until then, Melbourne was one of the few cities in the world without a Sunday newspaper: 'The Melbourne Sunday was world famous,' he wrote in his book *Wowsers*, 'a tourist attraction really, like trams and 6 o'clock closing. Where else on earth, with the possible exception of Adelaide, could you find a city where absolutely nothing happened?' Actually, there was such a place: Perth. In 1972 an Indian prince, Mukarram Jah, the Nizam of Hyderabad, immigrated to Western Australia. He and his offsider spent their first night in a Perth hotel, then, next morning, decided to walk outdoors in the Sunday morning sunshine. According to his biographer, John Zubrzycki, they found the streets entirely empty of people, so much so they formed the view that martial law had been declared. They retreated rapidly back to their hotel.

Meanwhile, in New South Wales, they were going wild: the Sunday Observance Act was repealed in 1966, which meant you could henceforth attend the cinema EVEN BEFORE EVENSONG.

10. You couldn't eat outdoors in all of Queensland

Canberra was not the only place in which outdoor eating was banned in all cafés and restaurants. In Queensland, the law was not changed until 1988 when, as part of the crazy, celebratory atmosphere of the World Expo, the government threw caution to the wind and allowed cafés to temporarily serve food in the open air. It proved a slippery slope, and soon Queenslanders were regularly munching sandwiches in the sun – a practice they scandalously maintain to this day. Why had it been banned in the first place? According to Sallyanne Atkinson, the lord mayor of Brisbane at the time, authorities had been worried by the health dangers posed by flies.

*

Have my Top Ten Improvements convinced you? The crime figures alone are pretty good, I like to think; plus, the way you are living so much longer should garner some appreciation. We should be happy! Yet optimism is often regarded as a bit soft-minded. And after so much optimism in this chapter, I'm sure every reader will have a 'yes … but'. Here's my attempt to pre-empt three of the 'yes … buts' that might be in your mind.

'Yes … but there's greater economic inequality'

Fair cop, at least for Australia. The OECD uses something called the GINI coefficient to measure how fairly income is shared. Using this measure alongside some taxation data, Australia was very unequal in the early 1950s (partly because the wool boom created some momentarily wealthy graziers). Income then steadily became more equal as we headed towards and through the 1970s. By about 1979, we were at peak equality. Then inequality started to grow again, reaching a high just before the global financial crisis of 2008. Since then, we have become a little more equal – but nowhere near the level we achieved in the late 1970s.

The complication, of course, is that while the rich are getting richer, it's also true that the poor are getting richer. Comparing people living in poverty – 1970 vs now – is difficult: the Henderson Poverty Line was used to measure such matters in the '60s and '70s but, more recently, different methods have been adopted. It's hard to find an accepted index that allows a fair comparison. Professor Roger Wilkins is from the Melbourne Institute, which was home to the Henderson Poverty Line. In 1975, Henderson estimated that 8.2 per cent of the Australian population was below the poverty line, then set at $62.70 per week for a family of four. Professor Wilkins says that, adjusted for inflation, that poverty line is about $560 per week at 2018 prices. He estimates that about 1.5 per cent of people would be below that poverty line today. His conclusion:

> There is good evidence that all boats have risen – the poor today are, broadly speaking, better off in terms of material wellbeing, even allowing for rising housing costs. This is further reinforced by the expansion of public

health care that has occurred since the early 1970s. Of course, we know relativities really do matter (a lot), so it is entirely possible that the poor in modern Australia feel considerably worse off than the poor in 1960s and 1970s Australia. To be able to 'participate' in modern Australian society requires substantially more resources than it did in the 1960s.

He also notes the general increase in income levels.

The big change was between 1993 and 2008, which saw extraordinary real growth in household incomes. There wasn't much growth before that [from the mid-1970s] and there has been essentially no growth since then. Overall, in real terms, average incomes are about 70% higher now than in the mid-1970s.

Internationally, the situation is similar. It's true the rich are getting richer – the world's eight richest individuals control the same wealth, according to Oxfam, as the world's poorest half. Yet at the same time, as Steven Pinker points out, poverty is shrinking dramatically. As he has put it: 'Newspapers could have printed the headline "Number of People in Extreme Poverty Fell by 137,000 Yesterday" every day for the last 25 years and been correct on every occasion.'

We should be outraged by the world's continuing inequality – but couldn't we also acknowledge a statistical truth: nearly everyone is better off.

'Yes ... but we're less charitable'

Probably not true. I've tried to find some figures from the 1960s, but they are elusive. We are less religious, but does that mean less giving? All I can find is a 2017 study from the Queensland University of Technology, using tax department data from 1978 onwards. Its conclusion? 'Donations made by Australian taxpayers far exceed inflation as measured by the Consumer Price Index ... the total amount donated is at its highest point ever.'

'Yes ... but the music was better'

Fair call. Completely agree.

*

An army of the aggrieved has taken up residence in Australia and no one is game to tell them the truth: life in Australia, right now, right here, is better than it used to be. No one wants to mumble this sunny truth because it's so much easier to pander to the pessimistic and indulge in deluded nostalgia.

Besides which, if you don't pander, if you tell the optimistic truth, you are quickly slapped down: 'You just don't understand,' or 'That just proves how out of touch you are.' Then out comes the wagging finger: 'You should try being Aboriginal.' Or young. Or old. Or gay. Or a refugee on Manus Island. Or a divorced dad done over by the Family Court. No one wants to stand between a fellow Australian and this hunger for victimhood. And so we end up with an echo chamber of discontent, in which every attempt at optimism is shouted down – the present always worse than an imagined lotus-eating past.

Australian elections in particular are occasions when the bleak inherit the Earth. It's hard to get through the day without hearing a candidate quote some miserable but unlikely statistic. 'More than 48 per cent of Australians are functionally illiterate,' someone said during an election panel I chaired a few years back and – I confess – I didn't have the courage to say, 'That seems a little unlikely.' Who wants to be the person insufficiently outraged by functional illiteracy? Who wants to be the one saying, 'Oh, cheer up, life can't be that bad.'

No one seems to recall A.B. Facey's book *A Fortunate Life*. Have we no memory of the horrors faced – then optimistically shrugged off – by a previous generation of Australians? Do any of the angry people who voted for Pauline Hanson, insisting on a return to the 'good old days', remember the past recounted by Albert Facey – two world wars and a terrifying Depression? And yet, still he talked of his 'fortunate life'.

It's not only the unhappy, old white men of One Nation. On ABC TV in 2016, a team of youthful reporters presented a program called *The War on Young People*. Again, the army of the aggrieved was on the march. Some good points were made. For today's young there's a crisis in housing affordability, an uncertain job market and the burden of student loans. Throw in the new liquor licensing laws in Sydney's CBD – which killed off some of the nightlife – and, bingo, there's your war on young people.

Fair enough. On the other hand, I'd rather be female now than in the Australia of the past. I'd rather be gay now. I'd also rather be heterosexual – freed from the gender straitjackets of my adolescence. And, of course, I'd rather be a 19-year-old now than in 1970, facing conscription and the possibility of death in Vietnam. Not so much 'The War on Young People'; rather 'The Young People Sent to War'.

Life, I say, with great trepidation, has its up and downs. Each generation faces its particular hardships. Where did this myth of perpetual decline come from? The notion that we must pretend that life used to be better when it clearly wasn't? Being aggrieved can, of course, be a good thing; it can be the force that makes the world a better place. But – for individuals and for nations – it can also strip us of happiness, momentum and even ambition. Why try to achieve change when everything and everybody is so clearly against you?

It's not only Australia that has developed this taste for pessimism. In his book, *Enlightenment Now*, Steven Pinker writes about Americans who simply refuse to believe the optimistic truth. It cannot be right, they say, that crime is down; or that war is less common than it was; or that the number of people living in poverty is lower with each passing day. Pinker – who presents his proof in a blizzard of charts – blames the Internet-charged ubiquity of the news media and its tendency to emphasise the negative, alongside a bias towards anxiety in the human brain.

He quotes some American opinion polling: in almost every year from 1992 to 2015 – an era in which the rate of violent crime plummeted – a majority of Americans told pollsters that crime was rising. In most of the last 40 years – years marked by dramatic rises in longevity and affluence – a solid majority of Americans have told pollsters that the country is 'heading in the wrong direction'. He notes that the recent Pulitzer non-fiction prizes were given to 'four books on genocide, three on terrorism, two on cancer and one on extinction'.

The same point is made by the Swedish writer and statistician Hans Rosling in his book *Factfulness*, published shortly before his death in 2017. When he surveyed people about the state of the world, they were, on average, much more pessimistic than the data warranted. Most people, for example, thought extreme poverty was either unchanged over the last 20 years or had actually risen. The truth is, it has tumbled remarkably. To quote Rosling's data: in 1966, half the world's population lived on less than $2 a day (in 2017 money). By 1997, that had fallen to 29 per cent and, by 2017, to 9 per cent. The past five years, Rosling wrote in 2017, had been the greatest five-year period in history in terms of reducing child mortality.

Nostalgia for the past infects both left and right. According to a recent Lowy Institute Poll, 79 per cent of Australians say they are dissatisfied about 'the way things are going in the world today'. The Australian novelist D.B.C. Pierre calls it 'declinism – the belief that things are getting worse'. It is, he has said, 'what happens as we age and our youths grow much rosier in our minds'. Some say the aging population is the problem, although the young appear to be almost as bad as their parents. A 2018 Deloitte survey of Australian millennials found that two-thirds believe politicians have a negative impact on society. That's not just politicians from one side or the other – that's all politicians.

The urge to make the world a better place does, it's true, involve being angered by the problems of today. Plenty of politicians *are* terrible; there *are* many threats to our happiness. But, sometimes, progress can also be served by celebrating how far we've come. The world of 1970s Australia is almost unimaginable in its level of legal prejudice and casual brutality; its sexism, racism and homophobia. To appreciate how bad things were, and yet how quickly things changed, can embolden us.

Change is possible. Having done it once, we can do it again. We are not stuck with what we have. Much of the society we have today – the continuing inequality and discrimination – will, one day, seem as peculiar as the '70s appears now.

During that era, many ideas appeared to be set in stone – 'just part of human nature'. They were later jettisoned as appalling, unconceivable, immoral. People who drove those changes were, at the time, often viewed as ridiculous and foolish. They were later cheered on as heroes.

That so much of this edifice of unfairness has been dismantled, and in such a short time, should be a matter of inspiration. As Steven Pinker (okay, I know I'm overquoting him) puts it: 'The point of calling attention to progress is not self-congratulation but identifying the causes so we can do more of what works.'

Australia, in recent decades, has turned its back on its sleepy past. It's hosted a bold experiment. What would happen if a country opened itself up to the world – inviting immigration from everywhere, pulling down trade walls, floating its dollar, attempting to live on its wits as well as its minerals? The result has been the building of one of the most successful countries on earth – the only Western economy to avoid recession for the best part of three decades; a country that navigated past the Asian meltdown and the global financial crisis; a place where, most of the time, people of many backgrounds really do embrace, learn from each other and prosper. Here's George Megalogenis: 'Even if we manage to revert to mediocrity, the Australian moment will be of interest for decades to come, as a reminder of what worked, and what might be.'

More inspiring still: all this was achieved within the lifetime of many of us. The 1965 starting point was an insular, frightened monoculture – 'a lucky country', in Horne's phrase, 'run mainly by second-rate people who share its luck'.

There's nothing soft-minded about taking pleasure in what has been achieved – achieved by leaders such as Charles Perkins, Gough Whitlam, Anne Summers, the brave men and women of CAMP, the anti-Vietnam marchers and the union leaders who, despite the temporary pain for their members, understood that we should not forever cringe behind a wall of tariffs.

Failing to take pleasure in what's been won is not only disrespectful to those leaders, it's also disrespectful to the rest of us – the people who applauded, who voted and who marched. The people who ate, and at the time enjoyed, the Spicy Meat Ring … but dreamed there might be something better.

We changed a thousand things. We stopped building our houses out of asbestos sheeting. We stopped forcing single mothers to give up their children for adoption. We started, most of us, to respect each other whatever our gender, race or sexuality. We cleaned the water and we cleaned the air.

More to the point: we now have avocado.

Bibliography

Broomham, Rosemary, *On the Road: the NRMA's First Seventy Years*, Allen & Unwin, 1996

Davis, Tony, *Total Lemons*, ABC Books, 2012

Deveson, Anne, *Australians at Risk*, Cassell Australia, 1978

Dunstan, Keith, *Wowsers*, Cassell Australia, 1968

Heiss, Anita (ed.), *Growing Up Aboriginal in Australia*, Black Inc., 2018

Horne, Donald, *The Lucky Country*, Angus & Robertson, 1964

Marr, David, 'The White Queen: One Nation and the Politics of Race', *Quarterly Essay*, 2017

Megalogenis, George, *The Australian Moment*, Penguin, 2012

Mackay, Hugh, *Advance Australia … Where?* Hachette, 2007

Mackay, Hugh, *Australia Reimagined*, Pan Macmillan Australia, 2018

McGregor, Craig, *Profile of Australia*, Penguin, 1966

Mundine, Warren, *In Black and White*, Pantera Press, 2017

O'Connell, Jan, *A Timeline of Australian Food: From Mutton to MasterChef*, NewSouth Publishing, 2017

Pinker, Steven, *Enlightenment Now*, Viking, 2018

Sewell, Elizabeth (ed.), *Miss Australia Cookbook*, Paul Hamlyn, 1971

Summers, Anne, *Damned Whores and God's Police*, Penguin, 1975

Zubrzycki, John, *The Last Nizam*, PanMacmillan, 2006

A Note on Sources

71   Merle Thornton, 'I'm prepared to pay...'; from an article on the ABC News website, published on 25 March 2015, marking the fiftieth anniversary of her Regatta Hotel protest.

138   Bruce Dawe, 'Homo suburbiensis', published in *Sometimes Gladness – Collected Poems 1954–1982*, Longman Cheshire, 1984.

197   Noel Pearson, 'We've made progress...'; from the ABC's *Q&A* program, 29 May 2017.

211   Dame Zara Bate, 'He doesn't really hate rabbits...'; from an article in the The *Bulletin* by Frank Moorhouse, reprinted in Moorhouse's book about the period, *Days of Wine and Rage*, Penguin Books, 1980.

211   Gerard Henderson's quotes come from my interview with him.

224   Ross Campbell, 'When we go to other countries...', published in the *Australian Women's Weekly*, 3 July 1963. It's also included in a fine collection of his columns, published under the title *My Life as a Father*, edited by Shelley Gare, Media 21 Publishing, 2005.

229   Donald Horne, 'The sacking of Whitlam...'; from Horne's *Death of the Lucky Country*, Penguin Books, 1976.

250   Max Newton, 'I've never seen $15,000 disappear...'; from Evan Whitton's book *Trial by Voodoo*, Random House, 1994.

257–258 The quotes from Professor Roger Wilkins are from personal correspondence.

263   The Lowy Institute poll was conducted in June 2017 and is published on its website: www.lowyinstitute.org

263   D.B.C. Pierre, 'declinism – the belief...'; from an article published in the *The Australian*, 6 October 2017.

Acknowledgements

I'd like to thank my youthful ABC colleague Mariam Chehab who, along with my sons Dan and Joe Glover, set this whole adventure in motion by their shared incredulity at some of my stories. Thanks also to friends, young and old, who have read drafts or allowed the stealing of memories: Arun Abey, Paul Andrews, Susanne Andrews, David Braddon-Mitchell, Philip Clark, David Chenu, Simon Cowap, Jurate Janavicius, Jane Lancaster, Kerrie Laurence, Julie Money, Serge Negus, Tim Perkins, Domenico and Anna Perri, Olivia Shead, Rick Stein, Sarah Stein and Rene Vogelzang. My life is made immeasurably better by my ABC workmates, Emma Crowe and Elizabeth Green, who turn every workday into a joy. The ABC's state political correspondent, Sarah Gerathy, also helped me, and, as always, I shamelessly stole ideas from my radio buddy, James Valentine.

I've also leant on many people's expertise, among them: Dr Don Weatherburn, long-time boss of the NSW Bureau of Crime Statistics and Research; Dr Simon Chapman, Emeritus Professor in the School of Public Health at the University of Sydney; Professor Rebecca Ivers, Professor of Public Health, Faculty of Medicine at the University of NSW; John Tyas from Avocados Australia; Anne Hollands, director of the Australian Institute of Family Studies; Professor James Franklin from the University of NSW; Professor Roger Wilkins from the Melbourne Institute; Dr Samantha Bricknell from the Australian Institute of Criminology; Gerard Henderson from the Sydney Institute; Gary Jaynes from the Australian Lesbian and Gay Archives; Dr Sophie Pointer from the Research Centre for Injury Studies at Flinders University; Christine Erskine and Stacie Powell from Kidsafe NSW; Dr Richard Franklin from James Cook University; Emeritus Professor Murray Goot from Macquarie University; David Brown from Driven Media; Peter Hartcher from Fairfax Media; Peter Khoury from the NRMA; and Associate Professor Wendy Scaife from the QUT Business School. Plus, of course, those two amazing social researchers of Australia, Rebecca Huntley and Hugh Mackay.

As always, I'm extremely grateful to Mary Rennie and Brigitta Doyle from HarperCollins, and, from Cameron's Management, to Jeanne Ryckmans, Jo Butler and Anthony Blair.

And, of course, Debra Oswald. My inspiration, always.

Also by Richard Glover

Flesh Wounds

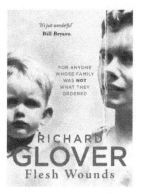

A mother who invented her past, a father who was often absent, a son who wondered if this could really be his family.

Part poignant family memoir, part rollicking venture into a 1970s Australia, this is a book for anyone who's wondered if their family is the oddest one on the planet. The answer: 'No'. There is always something stranger out there.

'A funny, moving, very entertaining memoir'
– Bill Bryson, *The New York Times*

The Mud House: How Four Friends Built a Place in the Australian Bush

A young man who didn't know HOW to be a man.

Two women willing to wrestle in mud.

A friend who knew his way around a set of power tools.

Building a house has never been so funny. Or life-changing.

'Hilarious' – *Sydney Morning Herald*

George Clooney's Haircut and Other Cries for Help

Richard Glover's deeply skewed stories create a world which is both weird and wry – a world in which Henry VIII provides marriage advice, JD Salinger celebrates tap-water and naked French women bring forth a medical miracle. It's also a world in which shampoo is eschewed, the second-rate is praised and George Clooney's haircut can help save a relationship. Bizarre yet commonplace, funny yet relatable, absurd yet oddly warm-hearted, in Richard Glover's hands you'll experience the true strangeness of the life you are living right now.

'Full-on, uncontrollable, laugh-till-you-weep stories.'
– Geraldine Brooks

Why Men are Necessary and More News From Nowhere

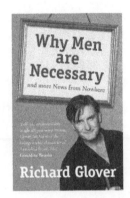

Funny stories of everyday life, as heard on ABC Radio's *Thank God It's Friday*. Meet the sexy and feisty Jocasta; confront teenage rebellion in the form of a fish called Wanda; do battle with magpies the size of small fighter jets; try to work out which font you use when speaking the language of love; and find out what men really have to offer. In Richard Glover's stories, the day-to-day becomes vivid, magical and laugh-out-loud funny.

'Glover is better than Proust. OK, maybe not better, but how often do you find yourself in a cold bath at midnight still chuckling over Proust?' – Debra Adelaide